The Literacy Hour and Language Knowledge

Developing Literacy through Fiction and Poetry

Edited by

Peta Lloyd, Helena Mitchell and Jenny Monk

David Fulton Publishers Ltd
Ormond House, 26–27 Boswell Street, London WC1N 3JD

First published in Great Britain in 1999 by David Fulton Publishers

Reprinted 1999

Note: The right of the contributors to be identified as the authors of this work has been asserted by them in accordance with the Copyright, Design and Patents Act 1988.

British Library Cataloguing in Publication Data
A catalogue record for this book is available from the British Library

ISBN 1–85346–578–X

Typeset by Textype Typesetters, Cambridge
Printed in Great Britain by Bell and Bain Ltd, Glasgow

Contents

Acknowledgements

The authors wish to thank the following:

- the staff and children of Grimsbury St Leonard's CE Primary School, Banbury, Oxon; St Lawrence CE School, Lechlade Glos; Barford St Martin First School, Wilts, and Dinton First School, Wilts;
- Ingrid Cleworth, PGCE student at Westminster College, for her work on 'Children Lost';
- Rachel Surman and Hayley Paintin of Westminster College for their tireless work in the presentation of the text;

We would like to thank the following teachers in particular:

- Sandra Findlay of Grimsbury St Leonard's CE Primary School;
- Kathryn Rees and Stephen Gibson of Barford St Martin First School;
- Yvonne Rayner and Sandra Crooke of Dinton First School;
- Sally Wrigley of St Edmund's RC School;
- Sue Read of West Witney CP School.

The authors also wish to thank the publishers and editors for permission to reprint extracts from the following copyright material:

Agard, J. (1993) 'If Only I Could Take Home a Snowflake', in *Din Do Nuttin*. London: Random House.

Burningham, J. (1970) *Mr Gumpy's Motor Car*. London: Johnathan Cape.

Crossley-Holland, K. (1987) *British Folk Tales*. London: Orchard Books (Reproduced by permission of the author c/o Rogers, Coleridge and White Ltd).

Fatchen, M. (1990) 'Children Lost', in *Poems Not to be Missed*. Australia: Magic Bean. By kind permission of John Johnson Pty Ltd. London, agent.

Hayes, S., illustrated by Helen Craig (1980) *This is the Bear and the Scary Night*. London: Walker Books.

Nash, O. (1990) 'The Adventures of Isabel', in *Poems Not to be Missed*. Australia: Magic Bean.

Noyes, A. (1981) *The Highwayman*, illustrated by Charles Keeping. Oxford: Oxford University Press.

Parkes, B. (1989) *Goodnight, Goodnight*, illustrated by T. Denton. London: Mimosa Publications.

Steptoe, J. (1991) *Mufaro's Beautiful Daughters*. London: Hodder & Stoughton.

Tolstoy, A. and Oxenbury, H. (1972) *The Great Big Enormous Turnip*. London: Pan Books.

Waddell, M., illustrated by Jill Barton (1992) *The Pig in the Pond*. London: Walker Books.

White, E. B. (1952) *Charlotte's Web*. London: Puffin.

About the authors

Lesley Ashforth

Lesley Ashforth is a Senior Lecturer in English at Westminster College, Oxford. She has a special interest in Language Study and Children's Literature and extensive experience in primary education as a teacher and deputy head teacher. Lesley was an advisory teacher for English in Buckinghamshire.

Ann Disney

Ann Disney has recently become Senior Lecturer in English at Westminster College, Oxford. She has previously been both Language Coordinator and Early Years Coordinator in primary schools. Ann has taught in Scotland, England and Canada and has a particular interest in Children's Literature, with a fascination for picture books.

Peta Lloyd

Peta Lloyd is a Literary Consultant for Dorset County Council. Previously she was Senior Lecturer in Professional Studies and English Education at Westminster College, Oxford. Peta has taught in nursery and primary classrooms.

Helena Mitchell

Helena Mitchell is Principal Lecturer in Language and Literacy and PGCE (Primary) Course Leader at Westminster College, Oxford. She has experience of early years education at class teacher and deputy head levels. She has published in the area of language and literacy and has completed research into early reading. Helena is currently leading a research project on gender and reading.

Jenny Monk

Jenny Monk has worked in primary schools in Birmingham and Oxfordshire. She was a deputy head teacher before joining the Primary Advisory Group for English (PAGE) in Oxfordshire. Jenny is a Senior Lecturer in English Education and Professional Studies at Westminster College, Oxford and has a particular interest in children's writing.

Mary Sutcliffe

Mary Sutcliffe is Senior Lecturer in Children's Literature and English Education. She has extensive experience of teaching in primary schools and prior to working at Westminster College, Oxford was headteacher of a small village school. Mary has also worked as an Associate Adviser.

Jane Talbot

Jane Talbot has recently joined Westminster College, where she is Senior Lecturer in Language Study and Children's Literature. Prior to this she held the post of Assistant Head Teacher with responsibility for coordinating Language at Key Stages 1 and 2. Jane has also worked with the Special Needs Support Team in South Wiltshire.

Introduction

The introduction of the Literacy Hour offers teachers the opportunity to develop focused work on texts to aid children's development as readers and writers, as well as speakers and listeners. The detailed schedule of the National Literacy Strategy (NLS) document provides a clear concise framework for the teaching of literacy.

In this book we have set out to provide a rationale for the teaching of language and literacy. This underpins the suggestions and ideas for teaching which form the main part of the text. We have focused upon fiction and poetry in order to deal with these aspects of textual range in sufficient depth. Thus, although some of the work trialled has included non-fiction, we have chosen not to include it in this text, in order to provide a clearer focus upon narrative.

The intention of the authors is that the book should be used as an aid to planning for teaching the literacy strategy. There can be no substitute for a confident knowledge of appropriate texts, but for those teachers who are still extending their knowledge of children's texts, we hope that the suggestions for teaching will provide an approach that combines learning outcomes and activities with the stated objectives at word, sentence and text level. It is essential that literacy teaching is developed through texts and not as a series of isolated exercises: 'Pupils must be working on texts' (NLS 1998, p. 13).

Teachers, students and the authors of this text have worked together to gather the practical suggestions in the book, which have been trialled within the Literacy Hour in schools.

Those involved in the production of the literacy strategy document have emphasised that teachers should plan from the objectives, as the use of any particular text may not contain appropriate material to meet the objectives for a particular term. Having selected and planned the teaching objectives, teachers have to select appropriate texts. We hope that the suggestions for teaching contained within this book will enable teachers to select appropriate activities based on the text. However, we would emphasise that not all suggestions for activities are intended to be used with each text. Rather, they should form a bank of suggestions for teaching from which teachers can select appropriately.

Teachers may also wish to revisit texts as they are teaching different objectives at different times. Such an approach would enable the use of the text for teaching as and when it was appropriate, utilising the objectives in a spiral and allowing revision of teaching as well as the introduction of new themes. This would need to be part of a whole-school approach to planning the Literacy Strategy, linked to assessments, ensuring that progression was achieved through the use of different texts at different times.

In suggesting the range of text-based activities outlined in the book, we have tried to take account of these issues, with teaching activities across the primary age range. We have also included ideas for work across mixed age range classes, as this is an issue which particularly concerns classroom teachers. Thus several texts have more than one grid, showing how the text can be used to meet the objectives for teaching a mixed age range class. Some grids incorporate objectives and activities appropriate to more than one term

Bibliographies enabling teachers to identify easily those texts which have been used have also been included. We used both big books (with enlarged text) and those with usual sized print. Although big books are an ideal vehicle for shared reading with the whole class, literacy strategy activities can be undertaken through the use of duplicate copies of individual texts, especially when working with older and more experienced readers. Teachers may also wish to make use of extracts on overhead projector transparencies when working with older children.

In suggesting these activities based on selected texts, we have tried to provide ideas that can be used by teachers for shared and guided reading, writing and independent tasks during the Literacy Hour, at all three levels of the strategy. Where an activity has been developed, it is outlined in more detail and the symbol '*' appears alongside the objectives. However, these are not just a collection of ideas for teachers: they form part of an overall approach to the teaching of language and literacy. The philosophy underlying this approach is discussed in the following chapter.

1 Planning activities based on a text: a process model

It is essential in planning for the Literacy Hour that important principles which have informed good practice, and which underpin the National Curriculum for English, are not lost.

> To foster in pupils a love of literature, to encourage their awareness of its unique relationship to human experience and to promote in them a sense of excitement in the power and potential of language can be one of the greatest joys of the English teacher. It is also one of the greatest challenges. (DES 1989, Chapter 7:7.3)

Emphasising the symbiotic relationship between reading and writing, the Cox Report (DES 1989) stressed the need to develop children's 'creative responses' to literature and argued that the experience of writing about texts 'leads also to an increased critical awareness of literary technique in the work of others' (Chapter 7: 7.9). That we should be concerned with developing such critical awareness and understanding while extending children's command of their writing repertoire is vitally important and this should not be confined to the Key Stage 2 classroom: the youngest children in our nursery and primary schools are capable of meeting the highest of expectations.

In a recent Radio 4 interview Richard Hoggart said that 'the book is the greatest creative encounter between two people'. While it is not the intention here to discuss the value of literature, it is important that we do not undervalue the power it has in people's lives. It is, therefore, essential that when working with literary texts we create a receptive context in which there is an opportunity for creative response.

Fundamental to any effective teaching of the literacy curriculum is the teacher's knowledge and understanding of a wide range of books for children. The teacher who reads children's books regularly, and who derives pleasure and satisfaction from that reading, is well placed to make informed decisions about which texts to introduce to her class. There is a need for regular reading and reflection, and for discussion of books and sharing of knowledge with colleagues. This is often done in an informal way but some schools have successfully established regular meetings, once or twice a term, when staff introduce new books so that a bank of knowledge is accumulated. This has the added benefit of contributing to the staff's sense of being a community of readers, an appropriate background for the teaching of reading. Against such a background, the focused work on texts can be both informed and reflective.

What follows, therefore, is a process model which will enable teachers to ensure that the integrity of the text is not lost in the search for practical ideas through which to develop children's literacy skills. It focuses on the teaching of the text and ways of achieving objectives from the NLS framework and will form part of an overall planning procedure.

Stage 1

Read text at your own level, exploring and considering your own response.

This is an essential part of the reading process and will enable you to understand the effect of the text and the nature of the demands made of the reader. Its importance cannot be overestimated.

Stage 2

Identify what the book has to offer children: what does this text teach?

This must go beyond the functional and beyond the NLS requirements. Your own reading will enable you to consider the effect the book might have, the possible responses which might emerge, and what the text teaches children about reading. Two sources of information are particularly helpful when identifying the distinctive features of texts: the levels identified in the Cox Report, included below, and the framework in Aidan Chambers' book, *Tell Me: Children, Reading and Talk* (1994). (It must be emphasised that Chambers' framework is intended for use with groups of readers but the preparation required for this demands close attention to the text and careful selection of questions from the framework. Consideration of these questions can, in turn, help teachers to identify particular areas of interest.)

Levels identified by Cox

- *Narrative:* Being aware of the story, particularly how it is sequenced; being able to follow the book at the level of its story;
- *Symbolic level:* being aware of what the story stands for – the universal meanings, and circumstances illustrated by the particular narrative; being aware of the metaphors and imagery used in the construction of the narrative and the descriptive passages;
- *Stylistic/linguistic:* being aware of the 'crafting' of the book, selection of literary devices and vocabulary, use of syntactic conventions; developing a critical awareness of the relationship between form and content (DES 1989, Appendix 6).

By considering each of these within texts it is possible to identify patterns at whole-text, sentence and word level so that you are aware of the choices the author has made and can prepare to help children develop their awareness and understanding. Table 1.1 provides a checklist which will help with this stage of the process.

These lists are not exhaustive, nor should they be seen as mutually exclusive. There are, of course, overlaps, and choices in one area will have an effect on others. For instance, when an author decides to tell a story through diary entries, it is likely that the first person will be used and s/he will make grammatical and lexical choices according to the nature of the teller – age, gender, circumstances, etc. Presentation, the way the words are arranged on the page, will obviously be affected, and font – style or size – may be used to create a particular impression. (See, for instance, *Dear Greenpeace*, Simon James, *Eleanor, Elizabeth*, Libby Gleeson, or *The Deathwood Letters*, Hazel Townsend.)

Table 1.1 The choices authors make

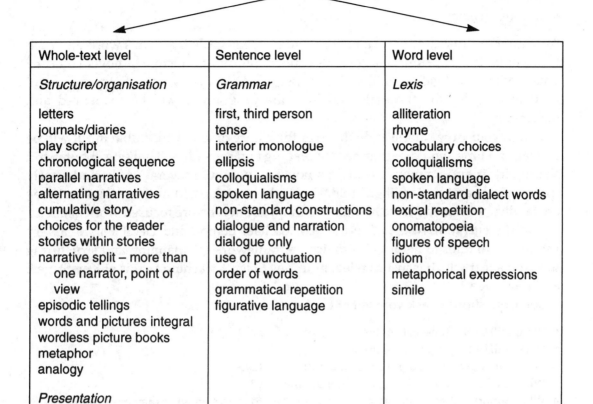

Content and genre

Whole-text level	Sentence level	Word level

Structure/organisation
 	
letters
journals/diaries
play script
chronological sequence
parallel narratives
alternating narratives
cumulative story
choices for the reader
stories within stories
narrative split – more than
   one narrator, point of
   view
episodic tellings
words and pictures integral
wordless picture books
metaphor
analogy
 	
Presentation
comic strip
pop-up books
flap books
pictorial novels
words and pictures integral
punctuation
choice of font – style and size
foregrounding of text (e.g.
   highlighting,
   capitalisation)
arrangement of text on the
   page
use of borders to frame text
	Grammar
	
	first, third person
	tense
	interior monologue
	ellipsis
	colloquialisms
	spoken language
	non-standard constructions
	dialogue and narration
	dialogue only
	use of punctuation
	order of words
	grammatical repetition
	figurative language
		Lexis
		
		alliteration
		rhyme
		vocabulary choices
		colloquialisms
		spoken language
		non-standard dialect words
		lexical repetition
		onomatopoeia
		figures of speech
		idiom
		metaphorical expressions
		simile

Stage 3

Creating a receptive context for the book.

For each individual book, what does this involve? How might it fit into a sequence or programme of work? For instance, work on traditional tales will vary in terms of focus at different stages and might involve ideas such as the following:

- traditional nursery tales (e.g. *The Three Little Pigs, Puss in Boots, Goldilocks and the Three Bears, Jack and the Beanstalk*);
- versions of the same tale from around the world;
- comparison of picture-book versions of the same tale;

- tales from one country or continent (e.g. British folk and fairy tales);
- tales on a theme (e.g. giants, tricksters, transformations);
- comparisons of the same tale presented in different media (e.g. book, video, audiotape);
- stories with strong protagonists;
- modern retellings.

An author or illustrator's work may provide a focus for half a term's work and each text will be taught within that overall context. Study of a historical novel could be linked with investigation of the relevant period. As with any unit of work, you will need to consider the timescale and how the programme will be sequenced and developed.

Within your programme and whatever the choice of text, your initial input will be crucial, and time should be planned for reading and re-reading it, talking about it and sharing ideas and opinions. Reading a novel may require several weeks and clearly this requires careful planning. Children should be immersed in the text so that they are familiar with it and have had time to think about it before focused work begins.

Teaching Literature Nine to Fourteen, by Michael Benton and Geoff Fox, is a very useful text to refer to here, as it provides a framework for planning and structuring work on a text which is just as relevant to Key Stage 1 teaching as it is at Key Stage 2 and Key Stage 3.

Some questions to ask yourself at this point:

- What will be the timescale of the overall unit of work?
- What will be the sequence of the work?
- When and how will you introduce the individual texts?
- What might you do beforehand to prepare the way?
- What opportunities will you provide for children to reflect on what they have read
    - in groups?
    - as a class?
    - individually?
- How much time will this work require before the focused work begins?
- What will be the outcomes of the work and how will these be presented to others?

Stage 4

Planning text-related work linked to NLS objectives.

Careful selection of texts will clearly be essential, and activities planned, which develop children's skills, knowledge and understanding, as outlined in the NLS. If features of the text have been carefully identified, then activities at each of the three levels can be planned for appropriately. Ideas for text-related work are described and explained in the following chapters and will show Stages 2 and 4 in practice.

Medium-term planning based on knowledge of a range of texts should ensure that objectives are achieved while providing children with varied experiences. Of course it will be important to consider planning for the Literacy Hour within the context of the whole English curriculum. Planning opportunities for development and extension of activities, including ideas for homework, will form part of your weekly and daily programme.

At the beginning of this chapter we emphasised the need to retain important principles and to maintain the integrity of both the text and the children's literary experience. The following questions from Benton and Fox's book will help you achieve both:

'Will this activity enable the reader to look back on the text and to develop the meanings he has already made?'

'Does what I plan to do bring reader and text closer together, or does it come between them?' (p. 127).

2 Picture books at Key Stage 1

This section looks at three picture books in detail:

- *Mr Gumpy's Motor Car* by John Burningham
- *The Pig in the Pond* by Martin Waddell
- *This is the Bear and the Scary Night* by Sarah Hayes.

For each book a rationale for its use in the Literacy Hour is followed by three grids which examine how the text could be used to fulfil text, sentence and word level objectives for a Reception class and one term from both Year 1 and Year 2. Grids have been organised in order for teachers to use texts with Reception to Year 2 children in year groups or mixed aged classes.

Most of the activities on the grids can be used flexibly; for example, an activity that takes place during shared reading or writing may also be used as a guided or independent group activity. Many of the activities would be appropriate for a large range of picture books, with some adaptation.

Grids A, B and C for *Mr Gumpy's Motor Car* and Grids D, E and F for *The Pig in the Pond* are followed by a detailed explanation of activities to use with the story at text, sentence and word level. Grids G, H and I for *This is the Bear and the Scary Night* are supplemented by lists of other books including bears as main characters and books with a night-time setting.

A list of suggestions for classroom activities related to each text gives examples for cross-curricular work which can be linked into the Literacy Hour.

Mr Gumpy's Motor Car by John Burningham

Mr Gumpy's Motor Car is John Burningham's second book about the affable Mr Gumpy, following the success of *Mr Gumpy's Outing*. The structure of the narrative is similar in both books. Mr Gumpy sets out on an expedition and is joined early in the story by an assortment of animals and children, which results in a considerable squash! The expedition proceeds well until a problem develops, when all are called on by Mr Gumpy to help. Despite initial objections to this, help is eventually given, the problem is resolved and the journey proceeds to its final destination, where all is happily concluded.

Each double-page spread of the book has a full-page coloured picture on one side and clear, bold text on the other. Most text pages have little print, accompanied by soft pencil sketches of the developing story. The black and white of the text pages balances the soft water-coloured pictures of the opposite pages with their larger scale figures and features of landscape.

As the story develops, the amount of text on each page increases, building up from one sentence on the first page to a dramatic climax enhanced by a page packed with text, which then decreases again towards the end of the story.

Within the NLS framework for range, the text can be considered under several headings. It contains language with recognisable and repetitive patterns, rhyme and rhythm. Although placed in a familiar setting, the plot is from the world of fantasy. The text is the work of a 'significant children's author' and contains a clear viewpoint with accessible themes and ideas throughout. The characterisation and plot are straightforward yet memorable.

The story is told as a third person narrative in the form of a sequenced recount of the day's events. The car proceeds in the reading direction from left to right across the page as the written text progresses. The story has a clear structure with opening, adventure and resolution. As a journey it is part of a common story theme.

The text makes use of simple sentence construction and the conventions of direct speech and inverted commas within the dialogue. There are opportunities to explore the use of apostrophes, comparative adjectives and -ed verb endings to form the past participle.

Text level work

1. 'Hold it in your hand'

Objective

- To choose and sequence the main points in the story through the 'hold them in your hand' activity.

Procedure

- One of the tricks of the trade of the oral story teller is to 'hold' the key points of the story in their hand, and children enjoy being taught how to do this. The story needs to be reduced to five main points for this purpose. This can be decided through discussion with the children, though it is useful for the teacher to have done the exercise herself beforehand. In the case of *Mr Gumpy's Motor Car*, the five main points could be:

  1. Mr Gumpy sets off for a ride in his car.
  2. The children and animals all pile in too.
  3. The car gets stuck in the mud.
  4. They all push the car to the top of the hill.
  5. They go home and swim.

Each point is allocated to one finger of a hand.

- The teacher recites the five points two or three times.
- The children join in, and when they can recite the points without the teacher, she instructs the children to close up their hands into a fist and says that they now hold the story in their hand.

This is a good precursor to the oral retelling of the story to each other, or to writing their own version of the story.

Grid A *Mr Gumpy's Motor Car* by John Burningham   Year: Reception

Text level	NLS para.	Sentence level	NLS para.	Word level	NLS para.
Understanding of print • Recognise printed words through shared reading and rereading • Use correct terminology to discuss features of the book e.g. cover, title, page, letter, word • Indicate directionality in shared reading and discuss individual words	1	**Grammatical awareness** • Teacher re-reads text with silly sentences – children identify the deliberate mistakes and discuss why they do not make sense • Oral cloze procedure: teacher re-reads text and stops at key words – children state the next word, using context to choose sensible possibilities • Discuss and indicate reading direction using a pointer	1 3	**Phonological awareness, phonics and spelling** • Talk about initial sounds in key words e.g. 'c' as in car* • Find other words that begin with the same letter, collecting these on cards in a 'can'* • Make a featured display of objects with names beginning with 'c' and label these*	2, 3
Reading comprehension • Read and reread the text • Discuss cues to help reading new words • Re-tell parts of the story to each other, sometimes using role play or puppets • Cover the text pages and read book using only the pictures • Discuss main events in sequence and 'hold them in your hand'* • Discuss favourite pictures • Draw a story map to develop awareness of structure • Talk about the 'Not me' page and think up more excuses	2, 3, 6 4, 5 7, 9 8, 10			**Word recognition, graphic knowledge and spelling** • Listen and look for key words in the story* • Match words to text*	5, 6, 7, 9
Writing composition/understanding of print • Retell the story with teacher as scribe • Illustrate key sentences from the text • Talk about letter sounds and formations as teacher writes • Write their own 'Not me' caption for a display* • Write sentences to match pictures from the story and compare with the original text • Plan, draft and write a thank you letter to Mr Gumpy after role play*	11 12 13, 14, 15			**Vocabulary extension** • Think of other possible words to extend the list of verbs when all the characters try to push the car up the hill* **Handwriting** • Practise the correct directionality for writing 'c' using different writing apparatus and varied activities in other mediums e.g. air writing, finger painting, sand writing etc.*	10 12, 13, 14

Grid B *Mr Gumpy's Motor Car* by John Burningham

Year 1 Term 3

Text level	NLS para.	Sentence level	NLS para.	Word level	NLS para.
Reading comprehension		**Grammatical awareness**		**Phonological awareness, phonics and spelling**	
• Read and reread the text	1, 2	• Teacher rereads text with silly sentences, children identify and discuss	1	• 'oo' as in 'too' 'ai' as in 'rain' these long vowel sounds are both found in the text and can be the starting point for collections of words with common letter patterns and for phonic games	1
• Discuss cues to help reading new words	3, 6	• Oral cloze procedure, children use content to supply missing words	2		
• Retell parts of the story to each other, sometimes using role play or puppets		• Teacher models reading with expression, taking account of punctuation, and uses open questions to raise children's awareness of the function of punctuation	3		
• Discuss main events in sequence and 'hold them in your hand'*	5	• Jumbled sentences from the text to be sorted and re-ordered	4	**Word recognition, graphic knowledge and spelling**	
• Draw a set of four pictures in the form of a zig-zag book to tell the main points of the story		• By discussing alternatives, look at the function of verbs on the page where the characters push the car	5	• Listen and look for key words in the story*	2, 3, 4, 7
• Play 'true or false' game (see *The Great Big Enormous Turnip* for details)	7			• Match words to text*	6
• Predict the content before reading, using title, cover, pictures		**Sentence construction and punctuation**		• Search text for words ending -ed and collect more for display and look, cover, write, check*	
• Compare with other stories about journeys, including *Mr Gumpy's Outing*	8	• Discuss use of capital for names and titles e.g. Mr Gumpy	6		
		• The first two pages of the story contain just one sentence in each – discuss whether this pattern is continued and how we know (full stops and capital letters)	7	**Vocabulary extension**	
Writing composition		• Examine use of question/answer language pattern*		• Think of other possible words to extend the list of verbs when all the characters try to push the car up the hill*	8
• Write a story about another adventure with Mr Gumpy in his car, using the same setting	12, 14				
				Handwriting	
				• Practise letter formations in conjunction with spelling patterns above	10

Grid C *Mr Gumpy's Motor Car* by John Burningham — Year 2 Term 3

Text level	NLS para.	Sentence level	NLS para.	Word level	NLS para.
Reading comprehension		**Grammatical awareness**		**Phonological awareness, phonics and spelling**	
• Read and reread the text	1, 2	• Read aloud with expression and punctuation, especially direct speech on the 'Not me' page (revise speech marks from Term 2)*	1	• Revise reading and spelling of words with initial consonant clusters and digraph 'ch'	1
• Discuss cues to help reading new words	3	• Substitute 'she' for 'he' in a rereading of sections of the text and discuss the result	2	**Word recognition, graphic knowledge and spelling**	
• Retell parts of the story to each other, sometimes using role play or puppets		• Add to the list of past tense verbs when the characters are pushing the car – do they all have the same ending?	3	• Listen and look for key words in the story*	4, 5, 8
• Read and compare with *Mr Gumpy's Outing*	4	• Compare with other words with the same root, e.g. push, pushes, pushing, pushed		• Match words to text*	
• Find out about the author and establish a feature display of other works	5	**Sentence construction and punctuation**		• Investigate suffixes -ed, -es, -ing in verbs*	7
• Talk about the difference between black-and-white pictures and the coloured pictures which do children prefer and why?		• Collect these past tense verbs into a list, using commas	4	• Investigate suffix -er in adjectives	
• Compare with other stories that take the form of a journey or outing and finish back home e.g. *Rosie's Walk* by Pat Hutchins, *We're Going on a Bear Hunt* by Michael Rosen	7	• Make a list of all who went with Mr Gumpy, using commas		**Vocabulary extension**	
Writing composition		• Write a sentence to annotate pictures from the story (this could be added to zig zag books)	5	• Think of other possible words to extend the list of verbs when all the characters try to push the car up the hill*	9
• Write a version of the story from the point of view of one of the characters, using a writing frame at the planning stage to establish the use of the first person pronoun 'I'*	9, 10	• 'May we come too?' – compare with statement form*	6, 7	• Talk about alternatives for 'squash', 'piled in', 'happily' etc. in context	10
		• 'Some of you will have to get out and push' – compare with question form*		**Handwriting**	
				• Practise handwriting in conjunction with spelling patterns above	11
				• Practise joins appropriate to the spelling patterns above	12

2. Story maps

Objective

- To develop understanding of story structure through story maps.

Procedure

- The teacher should model the drawing of the story map. (This can be prepared beforehand). The starting point for this story map is Mr Gumpy's house. The map needs to show the gate and the lane, the cart track across the fields, the hill and the river, drawn to show the circuitous nature of the day's outing. Drawings on the map can feature the main events at significant points of the story, for example, when Mr Gumpy meets the children and animals, all pushing the car up the hill, swimming at the end of the day.
- Children then draw their own versions of the map.
- Older and more able children can then annotate these, and the teacher can scribe annotations for younger or less able children.

3. First person narratives

Objective

- To develop awareness of story structure through retelling/rewriting the story from the point of view of another character.

Procedure

- Model the writing of parts of the story in the first person. A writing frame could be used, including unfinished sentences as starting points, for example:

    When I first saw Mr Gumpy in his car, I was . . .
    I said . . .
    On the way I saw . . .
    I liked it when . . .
    I did not enjoy . . .
    When we got back, I . . .

- Children continue the story with help or unaided.
- Written work can be discussed with response partners, or redrafted.

Further examples of first person narratives suitable at Key Stage 1 are: *Dear Zoo* (Rod Campbell), *A House is a House for Me* (Mary Ann Hoberman) *There's a Hippopotamus on the Roof* (Hazel Edwards) and *Wish You Were Here* (Martin Selway).

Sentence level work

1. Questions and question marks

Objectives

● To gain awareness of the question/answer language pattern.
● To understand the use of question marks.

Procedure

● Children sit in a circle. Teacher says to each in turn, 'Will you get out and push?' Child replies, 'Not me, because . . .' and gives his or her excuse or reason.
● This game also draws attention to the structure of questions; the teacher's question can be written on the board with accompanying question mark, and the punctuation discussed. Attention can then be given to the question early in the book: 'May we come too?'
● A wall display could be assembled around the question, 'Could you help Mr Gumpy to push his car?' Children could write their personal 'Not me because . . .' captions in speech bubbles to accompany drawings about this part of the story.
● Children could make up some questions about the story to ask a group of children 'in the hot seat'. The teacher should model some examples first, and these should be written down so that punctuation can be seen. Examples could begin as follows:

What did Mr Gumpy drive?
Where did Mr Gumpy go?
Who went with Mr Gumpy?
What was the weather like?
When did it start to rain?
Where did the car get stuck?
Who pushed the car?
What did they do when they got home?

2. Direct speech

Objective

● to develop understanding of direct speech.

Procedure

● Halfway through the story of Mr Gumpy there is a whole page of direct speech. This has great impact in the book, appearing as it does after several pages containing only one or two sentences. Discuss this page, drawing out points related to the punctuation.
● The speech marks can be named at this point, and described as the marks that show us the actual words that someone said.
● Children match the speech bubbles to the appropriate characters in the picture that accompanies this page of the text (see Figure 2.1).
● Cut out large card speech marks. Choose children to represent the characters from the story. These children stand in line in front of the class, and say the appropriate words. For example, the 'goat' would say, 'Not me, I'm too old'. As each character speaks, the teacher

moves along behind, holding the speech marks 'around' the speaking characters in turn.
- Draw the characters on to a work sheet. Children discuss and write something else that each character might say, and use appropriate speech marks. Take care that children understand that the reporting clause (e.g. 'said the goat') does not appear within speech marks if the children decide to use reporting clauses.

Figure 2.1 Speech bubbles

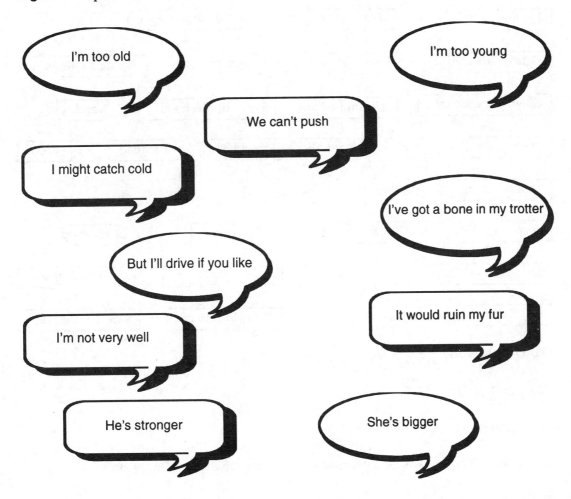

3. Jumbled sentences

Objective

- To learn about word order in sentences.

Procedure

- Write the sentences on strips of card and cut as marked (see Figure 2.2).
- Code each sentence on the back using coloured spots, to make sorting easier.
- The children collect all the pieces according to the coloured spots, then attempt to reassemble the sentences, seeing whether different combinations are possible.

Figure 2.2 Jumbled sentences

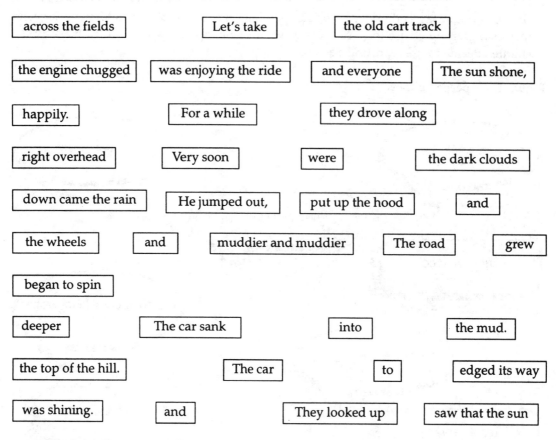

across the fields	Let's take	the old cart track
the engine chugged	was enjoying the ride	and everyone	The sun shone,
happily.	For a while	they drove along
right overhead	Very soon	were	the dark clouds
down came the rain	He jumped out,	put up the hood	and
the wheels	and	muddier and muddier	The road	grew
began to spin
deeper	The car sank	into	the mud.
the top of the hill.	The car	to	edged its way
was shining.	and	They looked up	saw that the sun

Word level work

Objective

1a. Word search

● To introduce/revise words, letters and letter patterns that appear in the story.

Procedure

● The following words can be found in the story. They appear in the Key Stage 1 Sight Vocabulary List, and can be used as a focus for a variety of activities aimed at instant recognition:

was	in	up
and	down	for
said	out	to
the	not	they

● Write the words on cards, with two of each word. Spread the cards out and find matching pairs. Read the words.
● With the same cards, the teacher picks up a word, reads it and asks the child to find another the same. The teacher turns her card over so it cannot be seen before the child starts to search, after a good look at the teacher's word.
● With the same cards, play 'Pelmanism'. This involves turning all the words over so they

cannot be seen. Children take turns to reveal two cards, trying to find pairs. If a pair is found the child keeps the pair. If a pair is not successfully found then the cards are turned over again before the next child takes a turn. The words are read at all stages.

- Make further copies of the words and play 'Snap'.
- Go on a Word Search. Working in a small group, each child picks a word card. The book is then looked at carefully. On each page the children scan to see if they can find their word written in the text. Keep a tally.
- Play the Apple Tree Game. Draw a large tree onto card. Make six red card 'apples' and number them 1 to 6. Place three or four word cards under each apple. Children take turns to throw a dice. They lift the appropriate apple and try to read the word. If they are successful they keep the word. If they are not successful the teacher says the word and the apple is replaced before the game continues.

The following words from the Year 1 and 2 list also appear in the story and can be used in similar ways:

another	but	came
don't	down	have
home	may	not
old	out	put
saw	some	take
there	time	too
very	way	were
will		

1b. 'Hold Up Your Word' game

This game is designed to teach instant recognition of the key words of the story. It will also develop the ability of children to listen with close attention to detail.

Procedure

- The children can sit in a group or circle. A circle is particularly good because then each child can see all other children and all other words.
- Make cards with the following words, written large:

Mr Gumpy	
car	clouds
the children	rain
the rabbit	wheels
the cat	hill
the pig	the dog
the chickens	the sheep
the goat	the calf

Enough cards should be made so that every child has a card. This will mean two or three duplicates of some words.

- Make sure everyone knows what their word says.
- The teacher reads the story, the children listen for their words as the story is read. When they hear their words, the children hold up their word cards, and then put their cards down again as the story progresses. The first time the game is played, the story should be read quite slowly. When they know the game well, children will enjoy the story read at a faster speed.
- Another development of this game is to give word cards to only four or five children. They

do not show their cards when they hear their words, only raise their hands. The other children in the class try to guess what words are on the cards. When all words are correctly guessed, the game begins again.

This game will help children to build up a vocabulary of words that they recognise quickly and automatically. It will also develop their awareness of the graphic features of words.

1c. Letter search

Procedure

There are many words in the story that begin with 'c'.

car	cat	calf
cart	came	can't
catch	cold	came

- Track these in the story. Make this the focus of a display of artefacts with names that begin with 'c'. Make word cards to accompany artefacts in the display.
- Find other words that begin with 'c' around the room and in other books. Make a list.
- Establish the correct directionality of 'c' for handwriting. Do this by modelling and 'air writing' (drawing the letter in the air). Reinforce by other multisensory methods, such as finger painting, tracing on the carpet, tracing on a partner's back, making the letter with plasticine.

1d. Words ending with -ed

The story provides a good opportunity for teaching the suffix -ed, used to form the past participle of verbs. When the car gets stuck in the mud, we encounter the following sentence. 'They pushed and shoved and heaved and strained and gasped and slipped and slithered and squelched.' This sentence contains eight verbs in the simple past tense, all demonstrating the -ed suffix. These verbs can be investigated in various ways.

Procedure

- Write out the sentence, omitting the verbs. Discuss what other words would be possible substitutions, maintaining the sense of the sentence and overall contextual meaning. What do the suggested substitutes have in common with the original words? The children will find that many of their suggested substitutions will also have the -ed ending.
- Highlight these words and discuss them with the children. What do they notice about them? Is there anything that they have in common? The children will soon identify the common letter pattern at the end of these words.
- Consider these words in relation to their root words and other words in the same family, as follows:

push	pushed	pushing
shove	shoved	shoving
heave	heaved	heaving
strain	strained	straining
gasp	gasped	gasping
slip	slipped	slipping
slither	slithered	slithering
squelch	squelched	squelching

- Talk about the differences they perceive in the way these words are used. Can they put the different forms of the words into sentences. What do they notice?
- Can the children make a collection of other words with -ed endings? Will they fit into the pattern of related words, as above?
- Look closely at the changes that some of the words undergo alongside the addition of -ed. Shove and heave both have a final 'e' in the root word, so only add 'd'. Slip has an additional 'p' before -ed. Can the children find anymore words that fit this pattern? Can they identify this rule? The rule is that if the root words ends with a silent 'e' preceded by a single consonant preceded by a single vowel then the consonant is doubled before -ed is added.

These activities will raise children's awareness of word functions, syntax and tense. They will also facilitate learning of the -ed letter pattern, for recognition in reading and for use in writing.

1e. Letter patterns

Procedure

The book gives an opportunity to consider the following initial consonant blends and digraphs:

sl	slipped	slithered	
cl	clouds		
br	bridge		
tr	track	trotter	
dr	drove	drive	
gr	gripped		
st	stopped	stuck	
str	stronger	strained	
sw	swim		
sh	shone	shoved	shining
ch	children	churned	chickens	chugged
wh	wheels		

Discussion of any of these can lead to searches for further examples in books and dictionaries, or collections produced by 'brainstorming'.

Classroom activities related to the text

Role-play corner

Establish this as Mr Gumpy's house, suitably furnished. Equip with road atlases, maps and picnic equipment to facilitate the planning of further expeditions.

Writing table

Children could write thank you letters to Mr Gumpy for their nice day out. Pin up a sample letter showing simplified conventions for setting out the letter.

Small word

Build a three-dimensional story map using small bricks and small-scale model houses, trees and figures. Reconstruct adventures with Mr Gumpy.

Push and pull investigations

Use cardboard or wooden ramps to test which cars will go furthest. Try them on different surfaces, such as wood, carpet, playground.

Model making

Use recycled materials to make a model of Mr Gumpy's car. Make the model travel by means of axles on the wheels.

Collage

Use felt scraps to create a landscape for Mr Gumpy's journey. Add a car cut out of card when the landscape is complete. Alternatively, paint the landscape first using soft colours with white added to give a watercolour effect.

The Pig in the Pond by Martin Waddell, illustrated by Jill Barton

(Before choosing to work with this book the teacher should be aware that any discussion of pigs may be unacceptable in Muslim and Jewish cultures.)

This book by Martin Waddell is a fine example of work in the picture-book genre. Throughout his work he has created characters with whom all children can identify in situations which are familiar to the child reader. *The Pig in the Pond* examines the child's need for adult approval. The anthropomorphic pig is very much like the child who knows that certain behaviours are not acceptable within her culture ('She didn't go in because pigs don't swim'), but sometimes the temptation of the circumstances (in this case, the cool water) can be just too strong to resist. The pig does jump into the water, causing joyful and riotous confusion; relief from heat, discomfort and the strait-jacket of behaving properly ensues. There is a climactic turning point in the story when Neligan, the figure of authority, returns from market. The reader, like the child, is not quite sure whether the pig's behaviour will be condoned or punished. Happily, Neligan behaves just as the pig has done, so everyone can relax, secure in the knowledge that good sense has prevailed over socially acceptable behaviour. The text indicates that sometimes it will be appropriate for the reader to defy convention. This is a powerful message for any reader and it is strengthened by the exuberant way in which it is presented.

Within the NLS framework for range this text can be considered under several headings. It contains 'predictable structures and patterned language' which support its use as a Reception class text; it has a 'familiar setting . . . with predictable and repetitive patterns', and it is the work of a 'significant children's author', which makes it suitable for inclusion at Year 1 and Year 2. It is also significant in that it uses features of traditional tales in its structure. It begins with 'This is the story of Neligan's pig' and ends 'and that was the story of Neligan's pig', thus enfolding the narrative within the storyteller's opening and closing tags.

Throughout the narrative, rhythm and repeating patterns of language demonstrate the text's affinity with features of the traditional tale. The book is a good example of third person narration and the visual text is particularly rich in the way it develops the narrative structure through its relationship with the written text. The layout varies

Grid D *The Pig in the Pond* by Martin Waddell and Jill Barton

Year: Reception

Text level	NLS para.	Sentence level	NLS para.	Word level	NLS para.
Reading comprehension/understanding print		**Grammatical awareness**		**Phonological awareness, phonics and spelling**	
• Use puppets to retell story	7, 4, 5	• Spot the difference: 'the pond's in the pig' 'the pig's in the pond'*	1	• Look at pig/big, find other words by analogy 'ig' on card plus some initial phonics – Can you make some new words?	1
• Sort and label farm animals using nouns written by teacher	1	• Teacher 'drops out' while children read repeating patterns	2	• Pond full of 'p's' for display – i.e. children suggest items and draw*	2
• Children hold up cards displaying name of animal as word is read	1	• Using prepared card, make sentences from a collection of words; sentences should match the one provided e.g.	3	• Find the phoneme to match with farm animals	1
• Class reread the story for puppet who has 'forgotten' how to read	1, 1, 10	The ducks went 'Quack!'		• Make animal alphabet books	3
• Discuss author/illustrator/title/page/cover	1	The geese went 'Honk!'		• Make new book titles e.g. The pig in the pond, The cat in the castle	4
• Highlight 'This was the story' 'That was the story' – discuss beginnings and endings	5	Neligan took off his trousers		• Experiment with onsets and rimes by cutting words up and putting them together again pig, hat, sun, pond, lot*	4
• Children find repeating sentences 'The pig's in the pond' or 'She didn't go in because pigs don't swim'		Neligan looked at the pig in the pond		**Word recognition, graphic knowledge and spelling**	
• Re-tell the story from a series of pictures	9	'The pig's in the pond'		• Work on high frequency words from text, i.e. and, on, the, went, in, all, was, – use lotto, pairs and snap games to practise*	6
• Listen to taped story	4			• Snap with animal names, 'Neligan' 'Pond'	5
• Make a class story map using first double-page spread – label locations, provide animals	6			• Fit words into graphic shape e.g. pig, in ☆	9
• Write labels for 'farm walk at Neligan's farm'	1			• Hunt the 'Splash!' words, hunt the 'pig' words	7
• Write instructions for getting to the pond	1			**Vocabulary extension**	
Writing composition/understanding of print				• Alphabet books } Make class	10, 11
• Teacher scribes labels for display, children dictate	11			• Information books on } collections	
• Discuss and make animal alphabet book	11, 14			farmyards } of new words	
• Children draw and suggest words, teacher to scribe, supporting children in prediction of graphemes				**Handwriting**	
• Write a shopping list for Neligan	11			• Painting water ripples for display	12
• Use concept keyboard overlay to create own version of the story	12			• Practise 'p' letter formation	14
• Use concept keyboard to create text for alphabet book	12			• Handwriting patterns in ripples to decorate alphabet book	12, 13
• Write shopping lists for use in role play corner	12			• 'ig' as a handwriting pattern	14

Grid E *The Pig in the Pond* by Martin Waddell and Jill Barton   Year 1 Term 1

Text level	NLS para.	Word level	NLS para.	Sentence level	NLS para.
Reading comprehension		**Grammatical awareness**		**Phonological awareness, phonics and spelling**	
• Use 'fallen words' techniques to explore contextual cues in first opening*	2	• Use sentence from first double-page spread but write words in wrong order.	1, 4	• First double-page spread – discuss rhyme and spelling 'dry' 'sky'	1
• Use 'fallen words' to explore tenses in first double-page spread	2	• Children to read and discuss, e.g. 'The sky shone in the sun' 'Dry was it'		• Make word list for other rhymes	
• Story telling as a class or in groups using Neligan's hat as a prompt	6	• Use 'fallen words' to explore tenses in first double-page spread	2	• Animal alphabet books, researching and making	2
• From a story map (based on second opening) retell story using stick-on characters	7			• CVC words 'pig' 'sun' 'hot' – writing the fallen words	3, 4
• Book talk	5, 2	**Sentence construction and punctuation**		• Blend phonemes in 'swim' 'quack' 'splash' 'shirt'	5
• During shared reading, children hold up sentence cards at appropriate points, e.g. 'The pig's in the pond' 'The ducks went "Quack, quack!"' 'Neligan looked at the pig in the pond'	6	• First double-page spread – How many sentences can we find?	5, 8	• Making plurals by adding s: 'ducks' 'fields' 'trotters' 'boots'	2
• 'Fallen word' – how many ways can we think of to work out what the word might be?*	1, 2	• Discuss full stops, capital letters, exclamation marks to end a sentence	6, 7	• Discuss irregular plural – geese	
Writing composition				**Word recognition, graphic knowledge and spelling**	
• As a shared writing opportunity decide on spelling for a 'fallen word'	8			• High frequency words from text: by, because, don't, his, water, out, were, took, next, that	9
• Book-making activity	11, 8, 10			• Snap lotto, graphic matching game, look – cover – write – check*	11
Non-fiction				**Vocabulary extension**	
• Make cards for Neligan's notes game; play the game as a class or in groups*	12, 14, 15			• Making animal alphabet books – finding unusual animals	12
• In shared writing activity generate prompt cards for role play or puppet play area	16			• Farmyard information	
• Draw up rules for role play area	13, 16			• Rhyming word lists	
• Plan posters for farm open day	13, 16			**Handwriting**	
				• Practise letter formation for each alphabet book page	14
				• Use pencil grips to support children who need them	13

Grid F *The Pig in the Pond* by Martin Waddell and Jill Barton

Year 2 Term 1

Text level	NLS para.	Sentence level	NLS para.	Word level	NLS para.
Reading comprehension • Book talk: discussion could focus on question 'Has anything like this ever happened to you?' • Draw story shape, discuss double climax* • Discuss and select animal poems for a class anthology; discuss sections, organisation of anthology • Make a true/false book, e.g. Neligan put his pants in the pond • Characters in role to tell the story, e.g. Neligan wearing his hat, Pig explaining what s/he did, Geese telling the story	6, 5 4, 5 7, 8 2, 3	**Grammatical awareness** • Look at past participle word endings in regular verbs 'looked' 'joined' 'gulped' 'gasped' 'turned' 'splashed' • Discuss 'because' as a linking word: 'She didn't go in because pigs don't swim' **Sentence construction and punctuation** • Highlight all the places in the text where '!' occurs. Discuss a class poster for using '!' • Highlight commas in the text – make a poster 'we use a comma when . . .' • Capital letter hunt – report back in plenary • Enlarge text only on first double-page spread, omit full stops. Children to add full stop in the correct place. Make a large full stop and attach it with Blu-tack	1 2 3 3 5 3	**Phonological awareness, phonics and spelling** • Final consonant cluster 'nd' • Work on vowel phonemes 'oo' – 'looked' 'took' • 'ow' in 'loud' and 'town' 'about' 'round' • Generate own word lists towards a pairs game • Revisit 'oo' 'ee' – make word wheels as a group activity **Word recognition, graphic knowledge and spelling** • Discuss past participle word endings in regular verbs • Speedy writing of high frequency words for test:* by, because, don't, his, water, out, were, took, need, that **Vocabulary extension** • Begin a class glossary of farmyard words (children to research from information book display) **Handwriting** • Patterns to match spelling: 'ou' (horizontal joins without ascender) 'ed' (diagonal join as letter with ascender)	3 4 1 7 7 9 10 12
Writing composition • Use 'The pig's in the pond!' 'At Neligan's farm, the pig's in the pond!' as a frame for own alternative section*	10, 12				
Non-fiction • Neligan has forgotten what to do before he gets in the pond; write instructions • Label map of the farm	15 17				

between full page spread and comic book-style framing, which acts as propulsion for the narrative. The pictures demonstrate characterisation through the use of colours and rounded, comforting shapes. The syntactic structure of the text supports young readers through repetitive patterns. The alliterative title might provide a point for discussion.

With the exception of the opening sentence, the story is told in the past tense. It is the past simple tense with frequent use of regular past participle -ed endings alongside irregular verb past tenses in 'went' 'sat' 'rose' 'came' 'was'. The tense also changes to the present in the passages of dialogue. This may be identified and discussed with interested children.

Text level work

1. Neligan's notes

Objective

● To explore imperative present tense and procedural writing; model behaviour of a writer.

Procedure

● In a shared writing session, children and teacher compose instructions for Neligan. The teacher explains how the finished sentences will be used in a role play activity. The 'notes' will be reminders for Neligan.
● The children suggest sentences which can be discussed, with particular emphasis on maintaining the present tense.
● The finished 'notes' form a role play activity where children choose a sentence from the collection, read it, and follow the instructions.

2. Story shapes

Objective

● To develop understanding of narrative structure of a story.

Procedure

Ask children in discussion to identify the points in the story where a turning point or something important happens. Draw the shape you identify together, e.g.:

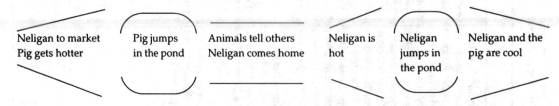

| Neligan to market Pig gets hotter | Pig jumps in the pond | Animals tell others Neligan comes home | Neligan is hot | Neligan jumps in the pond | Neligan and the pig are cool |

Use this shape in planning shared stories and experiment with different stories to see how many turning points can be identified.

3. Alliterative pages

Objective

● To develop awareness of semantic structure and rhyme.

Procedure

● Explore in discussion with the children the alliteration, rhyme and rhythm in a part of the text. For example, the frame might be:

'The pig's in the pond!'
'The pig's in the pond!'
The word spread about, above and beyond,
'The pig's in the pond!'
'The pig's in the pond!'
At Neligan's farm, the pig's in the pond!

● Use the passage as a frame in the creation of a new 'page'. Children will then demonstrate their understanding of the linguistic features of the text.

● The new version might read:

'The dog's in the ditch!'
'The dog's in the ditch!'
The word spread about to folk poor and rich,
'The dog's in the ditch!'
'The dog's in the ditch!'
At Neligan's farm, the dog's in the ditch.

This activity might be carried out in a group with the teachers as a scribe or as pairs of children working on their chosen animal.

Sentence level work

1. Spot the difference

Objective

● To develop visual discrimination and semantic knowledge.

Procedure

● Make a collection of sentences from the text, write them on card, then make some sentences which look very similar, e.g. 'The pond's in the pig', 'The pig's in the pond'. Close attention beyond the initial letter can be encouraged.
● This can be extended into a game of 'Does it make sense?' The children have to read carefully and sort the sentences into 'yes' and 'no' piles. These can be shared in the plenary sense.
● A further use for this kind of activity might be to look at graphic shapes of words and decide which one might fit, e.g. *pig* would fit in this shape ⌐▢⌐ but not this ⌐_▢⌐

Word level work

1. Pond full of 'p's

Objective

- To extend knowledge of initial phonemes.

Procedure

- Encourage the children to think of other examples of words which begin with the same sound as 'pond'.
- Children then research in alphabet books and dictionaries; draw the noun they have chosen; cut it out and stick it on the prepared pond which would form part of the classroom display.

A focus for the shared writing activities might then be differentiated and might include:

- teacher scribing for child who is being encouraged to predict the next letter from the sound she hears;
- child attempting own spelling and checking it in a dictionary;
- child choosing word from concept keyboard overlay;
- child choosing word from a series of words prepared on cards.

The pond which children have created can then become part of an interactive display where children can match nouns to pictures. This sort of activity can provide a good opportunity to demonstrate the stages of drafting through to publication.

2. Onsets and rimes

Objective

- Discriminate between onset activities and foster awareness of structure of consonant–vowel–consonant (cvc) words.

Procedure

- Choose a selection of cvc words (e.g. pig, bun, wig).
- Write them on card.
- Cut the word into its onset and rime (e.g. p-ig, r-at). Children can help with this activity.
- Encourage a group of children to see how many words they can create by reassembling the onsets and the rimes.
- Children should sound the words as they put out the pieces together.
- This activity can be differentiated so that one rime can be used with several different onsets (e.g. pig, wig, big, fig, jig, or pig, ran, rat, bun, etc.) and children can be asked to work in pairs with different onsets and rimes; discoveries can be reported in the plenary sessions.

3. High frequency words

Objective

● To learn the structure and the spelling of a focused selection of high frequency words.

Procedure

This needs to be seen as an enjoyable activity and can be linked to words as they occur in a chosen text. Children and teachers will develop particular favourites but several activities may operate during a session. Children will need to learn to play these games with adult support. They will soon be able to play alone. With a little imagination and forward planning the same sets of cards can be used for many of these games. If they form part of a pack they can be reused when the book is used again.

● 'Bingo', where children have a prepared card and teacher shows and reads the words;
● 'Lotto', where a base board of words is made and cards are placed face-down (or face-up) on the table. Children take it in turns to read the word and place it on their board.
● 'Snap', where words must be read as they are placed on the table.
● 'Speedy writing', where children read and practise writing a chosen word with great care. (This can provide an opportunity to practise handwriting.) Once the child can form the word, a sand timer can be introduced. The children have to see how many times they can write their chosen word before the sand runs out.
● Games with a die which has the chosen high frequency words written on the faces.
● 'Race', where high frequency words can be made from individual letters on individual magnetic boards. The children can race each other to see who can complete their list first. Lists might be read out by an adult, or a Listening Centre could be used.
● Children could be given a board arranged as in Figure 2.3 and asked to make 'I', 'and', 'the'.

Figure 2.3

4. Fallen words

Objective

● To explore rhyme in the text and to use knowledge of rhyme to predict.

Procedure

- Before beginning work with the children, cover up a selection of words throughout the text (e.g. on first opening, cover 'sky'). The words can be covered using 'Post-it' notes or 'Post-it' cover-up tape.
- When working with the children the teacher can explain that the words have 'fallen' from the page and we need to work out what they might be.
- In discussion, highlight rhyming words, make lists of those words and select the suggestion which rhymes and makes sense in context.
- The 'fallen words' technique can also prove useful when exploring other features of text (e.g. word classes).

Classroom activities related to the text

Display

Establish an interactive display with a copy of the text. Items might include:

- items of Neligan's clothing;
- labels which can be sorted to match the clothing;
- farmyard animals (models or photographs) with supporting labels;
- a sheet of blue paper labelled 'pond', containing a pig; children to be encouraged to add drawings of other nouns beginning with 'p' to be added to the pond;
- a sentence with blanks to add the noun, e.g. 'The ----'s in the pond.'

A selection of proper nouns can be written on card and placed beside the sentence.

An additional display could be focused on information texts and might take as a focus:

- farms;
- pigs;
- farmyard animals;
- markets (this could provide a rich resource in studying similarities and differences).

Role-play corner

There are many possibilities here which might include:

- the market which Neligan visits;
- Neligan's kitchen.

Writing table

Opportunities can be provided to:

- make shopping lists;
- write letters in role as Neligan;
- write letters in role as neighbour complaining about noise and mess;
- instructions for keeping animals cool in hot weather;
- newspaper report on hot weather.

Water play/science investigation

Find out what happens to water in a container when more items are added.

Small world

Provide opportunities for play with farm animals. A play mat might be used and a pond area designated for retelling the story.

Block play

- Building a new farmhouse for Neligan;
- making a plan of the farm.

Art

Experimenting with colour mixing in blue tones. This can lead to a class wall picture using the mixed shades of blue.

This is the Bear and the Scary Night by Sarah Hayes, illustrated by Helen Craig

This is the third book in the series following *This is the Bear* and *This is the Bear and the Picnic Lunch* involving the partnership of Sarah Hayes and Helen Craig. The boy and the bear go everywhere together, but one day, engrossed in his comic, the boy leaves the bear behind in the park. During the night an owl swoops and struggles to lift the bear into the sky. It cannot hold onto the struggling bear, who is dropped into the pond. The bear is retrieved by a park musician and, on returning to the park soon after with the musician, is found by the boy.

The story explores feelings of being left, lost, frightened, and found. The facial expression of both the bear and the moon watching from above highlight the mixed emotions which are endorsed by the speech bubbles running through the story. The illustrations generally spread across the double page and add detail and description to the text. Children enjoy finding the log and the dragonfly in the pond sequence, and tracing the bear falling through the dark sky from the top of the left to the bottom of the right hand pages.

Within the NLS framework for range this book can be included in the Reception and Key Stage 1 years because of its predictable and patterned language. It takes place in the familiar setting of a park and can be discussed in relation to other books in the series. Within mixed aged classes the text may be used to cover a range of Year 2 objectives, although it may not challenge children during shared reading.

The story is told through a simple cumulative rhyme. The written text is supplemented by the detailed visual text and comments, in the form of speech bubbles, from the characters. The opening leads into a double complication – the bear is left behind, the bear is taken by the owl and dropped into the water – both giving rise to speculation and discussion before the problem is resolved.

The rhyming couplets and predictable patterned language give the text a strong rhythm. There are opportunities for the exploration of sentence structure in relation to capital letters and full stops and also the use of the regular past tense.

Classroom activities related to the text

Role-play corner

Possibilities might include:
- the park;
- a 'dark' corner.

Grid G *This is the Bear and the Scary Night* by Sarah Hayes, illustrated by Helen Craig   Year: Reception

Text level	NLS para.	Sentence level	NLS para.	Word level	NLS para.
Reading comprehension/understanding of print • Track the text as teacher reads	1	**Grammatical awareness** • Teacher rereads text substituting 'girl' for 'boy', children identify and discuss	1	**Phonological awareness, phonics and spelling** • Through shared reading pick out words in text that rhyme	1
• Working in pairs, track the text with a partner		• Teacher rereads text substituting incorrect rhyming words, children hold up yes/no card if correct/incorrect	1	• Find words beginning with 'b' in the story, e.g. bear, boy, bed, blue, brave. Add more words to the list	3
• Teacher tapes individual and class reading of story, children listen to and follow taped versions	6	• Teacher rereads the text leaving gaps for the children to supply the rhyming word	2		
Reading comprehension • Read speech bubbles, encourage children to think of other things the bear might say	8	• Focus on repetitive sentence beginnings 'This is the bear who . . .'. Encourage children to find other endings to the sentence through investigating the pictures e.g. 'This is the bear who sat on the chair', 'This is the bear who said "I'm not scared"'	2	**Word recognition, graphic knowledge and spelling** • Make sentence cards containing words from 'b' word list	5
• Make bear puppets and encourage re-telling the story using language from the text	10			• Encourage children to read the familiar words, use book for picture clues, e.g. The boy wore a *blue* sweater. The *bear* was terribly, terribly *brave*	
Writing/understanding of print • Through shared writing, make new speech bubbles for children to read with expression	12			**Vocabulary extension** • Make a collection of key words that tell you what the story is about	10
Composition • Retell story and discuss differences between original and class versions, make into class book with illustrations	11			**Handwriting** • Practise writing letter 'b', make and collect b's, e.g. written, plastic, wooden, dough and plasticine	14

Grid H *This is the Bear and the Scary Night* by Sarah Hayes, illustrated by Helen Craig   Year 1 Term 2

Text level	NLS para.	Sentence level	NLS para.	Word level	NLS para.
Reading comprehension • Examine story characters. Make a list of characters. What does the story tell you about the characters? Examine a specific character's role in the story, e.g. boy, owl	8	**Grammatical awareness** • Substitute non-rhyming and inappropriate words when reading	1	**Phonological awareness, phonics and spelling** • List rhyming words from the text, e.g. bear, there; moon, soon; park, dark. Find and list other words that rhyme	1, 3
• Retell story and compare oral and written version	4	• Leave out/cover up verbs when reading, children predict appropriate word	2, 3	**Word recognition, graphic knowledge and spelling** • Discuss past participle word endings in regular verbs, e.g. look*ed*, scar*ed*, hop*ed*	7
• Discuss story setting. What other stories do children know that happen at night or take place in parks?	6	**Sentence construction and punctuation** • Look for sentences in text and find full stops	4	**Vocabulary extension** • Make a collection of words that describe the bear	10
• Compare books by the same author, do characters and settings reoccur?	5	• Demonstrate sentence building activities 'This is the bear who . . . ' using full stops and capital letters	5		
• Focus on dialogue in speech bubbles. What happens if only the speech bubbles are read? What else does the story need?	9				
Writing composition • Build profiles of characters	15				
• List main events in story and represent plot outline	14				

Grid H *This is the Bear and the Scary Night* by Sarah Hayes, illustrated by Helen Craig

Year 2 Term 2

Text level	NLS para.	Text level	NLS para.	Word level	NLS para.
Reading comprehension		**Grammatical awareness**		**Phonological awareness, phonics and spelling**	
• Class reading of text without teacher	1	• Develop awareness of the need for grammatical agreement by substituting 'girl' for 'boy' and following pronouns and changing the gender of the bear	4	• Explore vowel phonemes: *bear, chair, there* Add to list and split into three groups	2
• Read and compare with other stories that take place at night, locate key words and phrases that describe the night	5	• Re-read/write first sentence in the text	6	**Word recognition, graphic knowledge and spelling**	
• Consider how the night influences the bear's feelings	6	• for grammatical agreement, i.e. first person and past tense when rewriting the story from the bear's point of view	4	• Cover high frequency words from list with Post-it notes, children have to write word on Post-it or on own paper.	6
• Discuss the rhythm and rhyme of the text and identify the repetitive beginnings of sentences	9	• Children to read own writing to groups/class with expression	3	High frequency words in text: boy, who, his, would, these, might, man, home, made, his, there	
• Retell/rewrite the story from the bear's point of view	7	**Sentence construction and punctuation**		**Vocabulary extension**	
Writing composition		• Enlarge speech bubbles and rewrite/change text	6	• Make lists of antonyms, with the story as a starting point, e.g. dark/light, brave/scared, float/sink	11
• Use vocabulary collected from text and other stories set at night and write a description of a park at night	13			**Handwriting**	
• Make a 'missing' poster for the bear using text and illustrations from the story	14			• Practise handwriting joins in relation to: ar, al	14
• Use the rhyming structure of the text as a basis for writing different beginnings using substitute rhyming words, e.g. 'This is the boy who forgot his cat and left him behind in the house on the mat'	15				

Writing table

Opportunities can be provided to:

● write alternative versions of speech bubbles;
● write a thank you letter to the man with the slide trombone;
● write a description of the missing bear.

Waterplay/science investigation

Find items that float and sink.

Design and technology

Make a bear with moving arms and legs.

Small world

Design a 'park' story mat and reconstruct the story.

Art

Paint a night time picture including the bear and the owl.

A selection of books with a bear as the main character:

Jez Alborough	(1994)	*It's the Bear*
Stan and Jan Berenstein	(1972)	*Bears in the Night*
Raymond Briggs	(1994)	*The Bear*
Hans de Beer	(1996)	*Little Polar Bear, Take me Home!*
Debbie Gliori	(1996)	*Mr Bear to the Rescue*
Mick Inkpen	(1992)	*Threadbear*
Diana Noonan	(1995)	*The Best-Loved Bear*
Michael Rosen	(1993)	*We're Going on a Bear Hunt*

A selection of books set at night:

Janet and Allan Ahlberg	(1980)	*Funnybones*
Louis Baum	(1984)	*I Want to See the Moon*
Judith Kerr	(1983)	*Mog in the Dark*
Satoshi Kitamura	(1986)	*When Sheep Cannot Sleep*
Martin Waddell and Barbara Firth	(1994)	*The Big Big Sea*

A selection of books with bears as the main characters set at night:

Stan Berenstein	(1972)	*Bears in the Night*
Ron Maris	(1984)	*Are You There Bear?*
Jill Murphy	(1980)	*Peace at Last*
Jill Murphy	(1983)	*Whatever Next?*
Martin Waddell and Barbara Firth	(1989)	*Can't You Sleep Little Bear?*

3 Traditional tales at Key Stages 1 and 2

Traditional tales have reached us through the oral tradition, passed by word of mouth from one generation to the next. 'Traditional tales' include folk and fairy tales, myths, legends and fables. Children should have the opportunity to read and hear as many versions of individual tales as possible, so that they become aware of how stories change with each retelling, while retaining essential characteristics and patterns. Typical folk tale patterns include:

- settings in far away places
- timelessness
- simple plots where the same things are repeated
- fantastic events
- supernatural elements
- extreme characters – very good/bad, very fat/thin
- repetitive language
- the numbers three or seven.

This section looks at four traditional tales:

- *Goldilocks and the Three Bears* (retelling without text), focusing on Reception NLS objectives.
- *The Great Big Enormous Turnip* by Alexei Tolstoy and Helen Oxenbury, focusing on Year 1 and Year 2 Term 2 NLS objectives.
- *Mufaro's Beautiful Daughters, An African Tale* by John Steptoe, focusing on Year 3 Term 2 NLS objectives.
- *Jack and the Beanstalk*, in *British Folk Tales* by Kevin Crossley-Holland, focusing on Year 5 Term 2 NLS objectives.

For each tale a brief rationale for its use is followed by a grid which examines activities at text, sentence and word level. Some of these activities are then expanded in greater detail.

Goldilocks and the Three Bears – oral retelling

Goldilocks and the Three Bears, a well-known traditional tale, is a good starting point for an oral retelling of the story supplemented by appropriate sentence captions and character visuals if necessary. The predictable structure and patterned language are suitable for the Reception class, and for some children the story will be familiar. Printed versions of the story can be used for comparisons and alternative story language and illustrations – see, for example, those by Val Biro (1998), Moira Butterfield (1998), Jonathan Langley (1991) and Tony Ross (1991). The Grid overleaf outlines activities for Reception children.

Grid J   *Goldilocks and the Three Bears*   Year: Reception

Text level	NLS para.	Sentence level	NLS para.	Word level	NLS para.

Reading
Understanding of print
• Teacher tells children story using sentence strips (and visuals)
• Tape story for relistening
	1	**Grammatical awareness**
		• Captions are used to predict 'hidden' words, e.g. 'Who's been . . . my porridge?'
		• Captions are cut up, reordered and checked with original for sense
			2
			
			3
				Phonological awareness, phonics and spelling
				• Make a list of words that begin with 'b', e.g. a bucket of 'b's
				    a zig-zag book
				    an outline bear of 'b's
				• Discuss words that rhyme with 'bear'
					2/3

Reading comprehension • Children retell story with appropriate support, e.g. stick puppets, magnet board visuals, using appropriate language, e.g. 'Once upon a time . . .' • Children use sentence strips to read parts of story using appropriate expression	5 8	• Teacher retells story using incorrect words, e.g. Once upon a *crime* there was a little girl named *Goldisocks* . . .', Children point out mistakes	1	**Word recognition, graphic knowledge and spelling** • Find other books in the book corner that have the word 'bear' in the title, make a 'bear' book display	5
Writing/understanding of print • Through shared writing to rewrite beginning of the story and reread	11			**Vocabulary extension** • Make porridge and think of words to describe the taste and list these • Discuss words related to size of bowls, chairs and beds 'big', 'medium', 'small' and alternatives, make display	10
Composition • Children draw their favourite part of the story and dictate/write a caption • Captions are discussed and read • Class book compiled from shared writing/children's work	12 13				

Examples of story captions for re-telling

Type size relates to bear size. Picture prompts can be added.

Daddy bear

Mummy bear

Baby bear

Who's been eating my porridge?

Who's been eating my porridge?

Who's been eating my porridge and it's all gone?

Who's been sleeping in my bed?

Who's been sleeping in my bed?

Who's been sleeping in my bed and she's still there?

Who's been sitting in my chair?

Who's been sitting in my chair?

Who's been sitting in my chair and broken it?

This porridge is too hot

This porridge is too cold

This porridge is just right

This chair is too hard

This chair is too soft

This chair is just right

This bed is too hard

This bed is too soft

This bed is just right

Classroom activities related to the story

Role-play corner

Set up the area as the bears' cottage with appropriately sized bowls, chairs and beds.

Cooking

Make porridge with different textures and flavour. Encourage appropriate descriptive language when tasting, e.g. sweet, salty, lumpy, runny, hot, cold.

Small world

Make forest setting with bears' cottage, bears and Goldilocks. Encourage retelling of the story.

Design and technology / art

Design and make stick puppets of Goldilocks and the bears. Use in retelling the story.

Mathematics

Order sizes of chairs/bowls/beds using home corner artefacts or small world equipment. Focus on vocabulary related to size, e.g.

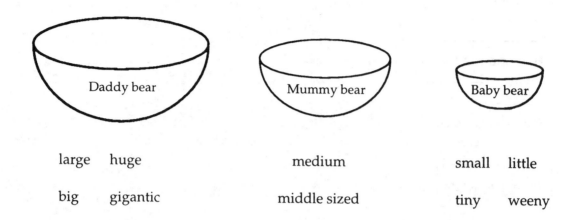

large huge	medium	small little
big gigantic	middle sized	tiny weeny

The Great Big Enormous Turnip by Alexei Tolstoy, illustrated by Helen Oxenbury

The Great Big Enormous Turnip is a version of the traditional tale written by Alexei Tolstoy. In this edition, Helen Oxenbury's stylish illustrations tell their own story. The text is confined to the simplest reduction of the narrative. The pictures spread across the gutter of the book, defining the spaces for the text without framing. Different perspectives are presented as the story develops: in some pictures the characters pull from left to right, in some from right to left; some pictures are close-ups, some are distanced and one is a bird's eye view.

The story is a cumulative tale. There is a problem to be resolved, and many are called on to come and help. This places the story firmly in the European tradition of folk stories. The pattern of the language in this story has many features of the oral tradition of storytelling, notably the strong pattern of repeated phrases. The repetition gives the story-teller time to pause for breath or focus on the next part of the tale.

The story can be compared with any other cumulative tales that the children may already know or can be introduced to. Children will enjoy talking about the similarities and differences. The following list gives some examples:

Pat Ealdone	(1973)	*Little Red Hen*
Colin Hawkins	(1990)	*This is the House that Jack Built*
Pat Hutchins	(1994)	*The Wind Blew*
Alfrida Vipont	(1971)	*The Elephant and the Bad Baby*

Within the NLS framework for range, the text can be considered across Key Stage 1. The language is predictable and patterned and can be read with a strong sense of rhythm. The characterisation and plot are straightforward and the illustrations enhance the words of the text. The tale has a clear sequence of events, suitable for oral

Grid K *The Great Big Enormous Turnip* by Alexei Tolstoy and Helen Oxenbury

Year 1/2 Term 2

Text level	NLS para.	Sentence level	NLS para.	Word level	NLS para.
Reading Comprehension		**Grammatical awareness**		**Phonological awareness, phonics and spelling**	
• Shared and guided reading	Y1: 1, 2	• Read text giving attention to punctuation, discuss strategies for reading new words	Y1: 1, 2, 3 Y2: 1, 2	• Orally discriminate syllables in words of one, two and three syllables that occur in the text*	Y2: 5
• 'True or False' game*	Y2: 1, 2, 4	• In rereading investigative alternative words that would 'fit'	Y1: 3		
• Compare oral version with written text	Y1: 4	• Teacher models proof reading and editing of draft writing before children attempt this themselves	Y2: 3	**Word recognition, graphic knowledge and spelling**	
• Compare with other versions of the story	Y2: 3, 5			• Listen for key words in text, e.g. pulled, called	Y1: 6
• Compare with other cumulative tales	Y1: 8	**Sentence construction and punctuation**		• Play word matching games (see examples related to *Mr Gumpy's Motor Car* and *The Pig in the Pond*)	Y2: 6
• Identify and discuss characters, build up character profiles using the pictures as initial focus	Y2: 6	• Draw attention to the use of full stops and capital letters in shared writing of the story	Y1: 4	• Use words in the text for focus on 'look, cover, write, check'	Y2: 9
• Retell the story to each other, sometimes using role play or puppets	Y1: 4	• Use spaces on the pages of this text to imagine what the characters might have said to one another, represent this by speech marks or speech bubbles	Y1: 5	**Vocabulary extension**	
		• Draw up a list of characters who helped and punctuate with commas	Y2: 7	• Build up lists of adjectives using writing frames*	Y2: 10
Writing composition		• Play the 'and' – 'but' game to draw attention to this construction in the story	Y2: 8	• Build up lists of characters	Y1: 10
• Sequence story using sentence strips*	Y1: 14	• Encourage the inclusion of and/but in children's written versions*	Y2: 9	**Handwriting**	
• Write own version of story with different characters, e.g. their own family, or with a different ending	Y2: 12, 13	• Use jumbled sentences to investigate word order*		• Words in the text give opportunities for practising correct letter formation and the four basic handwriting joins*	Y2: 12, 13, 14
• Write character profiles using writing frame for first draft to develop use of descriptive language, e.g. adjectives*	Y2: 12, 14				

retelling with or without the illustrations. The text lends itself to shared reading and the development of intonation and expression. Construction of sentences can be explored including the use of 'and' and 'but' to join ideas together.

Grid K highlights teaching objectives combining Year 1 and Year 2 with focus on Term 2.

Text level work

1. Objective

● To build up character profiles of the dog and cat.

Procedure

● Discuss the first pictures of the cat and dog.
● Use the writing frame (Figure 3.1) to draft ideas.
● Develop individual cat or dog profiles with accompanying portraits.

Alternatively, the work could form the basis of a retelling of the story with the dog or the cat as the main protagonist. The retelling might begin as follows:

> One afternoon the hairy black dog was snoozing on the sofa. He was dreaming about a large, meaty bone when suddenly the door flew open and the little girl called to him . . .

2. Objective

● To develop listening skills through playing the 'True or False' game.

Procedure

● Read the sentences below. After each one the children vote True or False.

> Once upon a time an old man planted a rose tree.
> The turnip grew up small and sour.
> The old man called the old woman.
> The old woman called the hamster.
> The black dog called the cat.
> The mouse pulled the cat.
> The cat pulled the old man.
> They never pulled up the turnip.

● Compare the sentences with the text.
● Children make up their own true and false sentences and play the game within a group.

3. Objective

● To organise the story into the correct sequence.

Figure 3.1

The dog looks

He does not want to help because

The cat looks

She does not want to help because

Procedure

- Write sets of sentences from the text on strips of card and cut them up.
- The children sequence the sentences in the correct order according to their recollection of the text.
- Sentences can then be matched to the order in the book.

As an extension, children can choose a sentence to write and illustrate; these can be joined together to form a zig zag book.

Sentence level work

1. The 'And' and 'But' Game

Objectives

- To establish familiarity with a particular sentence construction that is a feature of the turnip tale through the 'and – but' game. 'And they pulled and pulled again, but they could not pull it up.'
- To introduce compound sentence construction.
- The game will take children beyond the 'simple' sentence level and introduce them to compound constructions of sentences.
- This work can be extended through the 'Consequences' game.

Procedure

- Children sit in a circle.
- The teacher begins, saying, 'I went to the supermarket, *and* I bought some sausages, *but* I forgot the toothpaste.'
  The child then says, 'I went to the supermarket *and* I bought some toothpaste, *but* I forgot the bananas.'
  The game continues round the circle.

2. Jumbled sentences

Objective

- To investigate word order in sentences.

Procedure

- Write sentences on strips of card and cut as marked on Figure 3.2.
- Code each sentence on the back using coloured spots to make sorting easier.
- The children collect all the pieces accordingly to the coloured spot.
- The children attempt to reassemble the sentences.
- The children can then investigate whether different combinations are possible.

Figure 3.2 Jumbled sentences

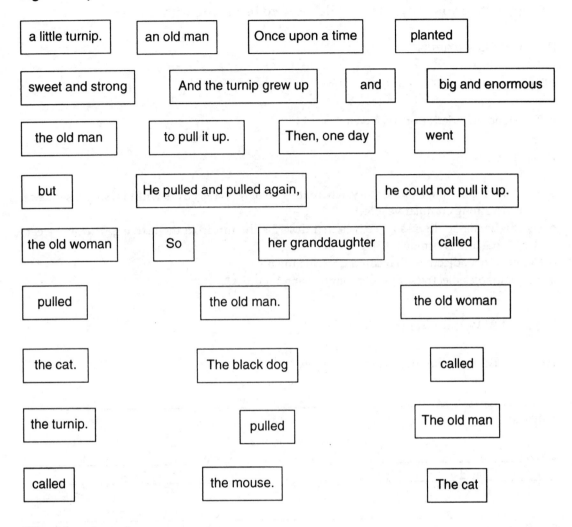

Word level work

1. Syllables

Objective

● To orally discriminate words of one, two and three syllables that occur in the text.

Procedure

● A search through the text reveals words of one, two and three syllables. Here are some examples:

One syllable:	man, cat, dog, mouse, big, strong
Two syllables:	turnip, woman, planted, little, again
Three syllables:	enormous, granddaughter

● Collect other words to add to these lists, starting with children's names.

A version of 'I Spy' can also be played, as follows:
  'I Spy with my little eye, a two syllable word beginning with . . .', etc.

2. Vocabulary extension

Objective

- To extend knowledge of adjectives.

Procedure

- Read the second page of the story, where the use of four adjectives within a single sentence creates a strong cumulative effect.
- Use Figure 3.3 to discuss adjectives that describe the turnip in the text, e.g. Turnip: sweet, strong, big and enormous.
- Collect other adjectives that could describe the turnip.
- Find suitable adjectives for other plants using Figure 3.3.

Figure 3.3 Writing frame

How would you like these things to grow?

Apples:

grow _____ _____
_____ and _____ .

Roses:

grow _____ _____
_____ and _____ .

Sunflowers:

grow _____ _____
_____ and _____ .

Strawberries:

grow _____ _____
_____ and _____ .

3. Handwriting

Objective

- To practise letter joins using words from the text, e.g.

  diagonal joins to letters without ascenders – as in *man*
  horizontal joins to letters without ascenders – as in *could*
  diagonal joins to letters with ascenders – as in *pulled*
  horizontal joins to letters with ascenders – as in *old*.

Procedure

The joins can be demonstrated at letter level before being put into context at word level.

Classroom activities related to the text

Role-play corner – design technology

Set up a garden centre selling turnip seeds and seeds for other vegetables, fruits and flowers. Design and make seed packets for sale, and other garden requisites. Special fertiliser packets and bottles could also have labels, describing their amazing effects.

Writing table

Make recipe cards with details of different turnip recipes. Make menus of turnip-based meals.

Science

Plant and grow turnip seeds in pots. Keep a diary week by week, detailing developments. Try different growing conditions and compare the results.

Sand play

Create a garden in the sand tray, with different designated areas, and recreate the story in this setting.

Mufaro's Beautiful Daughters: An African Tale by John Steptoe

Mufaro's Beautiful Daughters is a folk tale based on a story of how two sisters react in different ways to the king's search for a wife. Despite the brevity of the text, the language is powerful in its creation of place, characters and events, and is complemented by the illustrations. Themes running through the tale can be compared with those in tales already familiar to children, most notably Cinderella. Versions of Cinderella for comparison could include:

Cap O'Rushes by Alison Lurie, *Cinderella* by C. S. Evans, and *The Starlight Cloak* by Jenny Nimmo.

In Grid L we have chosen to ouline work appropriate to Year 3, Term 2.

Text level work

1. Objective

● To investigate traditional story openings

Procedure

● Collect examples of traditional tales, familiar and unfamiliar.

Grid L *Mufaro's Beautiful Daughters* by John Steptoe   Year 3 Term 2

Text level	NLS para.	Sentence level	NLS para.	Word level	NLS para.
Reading comprehension • Read story, read the opening and investigate the information it gives the reader*	1	**Grammar awareness** • Find adjectives used to describe the two sisters – discuss the function of adjectives*	2, 3	**Spelling strategies** • Use dictionaries to check meaning of unfamiliar words, e.g. yams, mullet, chanted, announced, transfixed, enclosure	6, 19
• Identify themes that run through the story, paying attention to illustrations as well as text*	2	• Make use of the adjectives in letter writing task		**Spelling conventions and rules**	
• Discuss the behaviour of the main characters – Nyasha and Manyara	5	• Investigate adjective/noun links*		• Word building using root and suffix – use term suffix*	13, 14, 16
Writing composition • Chart key incidents from the story	6, 7	**Sentence construction and punctuation** • Discuss the use of commas in relation to passage from text, use term in discussion*	6, 7	**Vocabulary extension** • Infer meaning of words from context, e.g. 'the air was *rent* by piercing cries'	18
• Use work on key incidents as framework for own writing, changing characters and events*	10			• Mufuro proclaimed to all who would hear him . . .'	
• Pretending you are Manyara or Nyasha write a letter to a friend describing the other's behaviour	8			• 'She stood *transfixed* at her first sight of the city'	

- Write out opening sentences and discuss with the children.
- Use the model grid in Figure 3.4 to highlight information given in various 'openings'.
- The children then compile their own grids (see Figure 3.5) from a collection of tales.
- Discuss similarities and differences
- A similar exercise can be used with 'endings'.

Figure 3.4 Model grid
Mufaro's Beautiful Daughters
'A long time ago in a certain place in Africa a small village lay across a river and a half day's journey from a city where a great King lived.'

What does the opening tell the reader?			
When	Where	Characters	Other information
a long time ago	in Africa	a great King	

Figure 3.5

Key incidents	Structure	Own version
Introduces village in Africa | Learn about Nyasha and Manyara | Arrival of letter | Manyara tries to get to the King first. Incidents in forest display characteristics of Nyasha and Manyara | Manyara warns Nyasha not to go to the palace | Nyasha meets Nyoka – green garden snake | Snake turns into King | King and Nyasha marry | Manyara becomes a servant	Setting | Introduce main characters | Something happens/ story complication | How main characters react to news/event What the characters do Happy ending: good triumphs over evil	

2. Objective

- To develop an understanding of story themes, e.g:
- rivalry
- jealousy
- good over evil
- parents unaware of situation between children
- obedience and disobedience
- kindness and unkindness.

Procedure

- Pick out themes from *Mufaro's Beautiful Daughters*.
- Discuss the main themes in relation to other known tales.
- Look for patterns and similarities. A list or grid could be devised which is added to during the term.
- Encourage the children to refer to the list when they are planning their own story writing.

3. Objective

- To develop an awareness of the structure of the story through listing key incidents
- To use structure in the planning and working of children's own story.

Procedure

- Make a list of key incidents on the grid on Figure 3.4 after reading the story.
- Discuss how the incidents are structured to form the story.
- Make generalisations of incidents on the grid in the 'structure column'.
- Use structure as planning tool for shared and/or individual writing.

Sentence level work

1. Objective

- To investigate the use of adjectives in building the characters of Nyasha and Manyara.

Procedure

- List adjectives from the text describing Manyara:

  clever
  strong
  beautiful
  sad
  worthy

- Add more to the list from developing knowledge of story and illustrations.
- List the adjectives from the text describing Nyasha's character and add to the list.
- Compare the lists, looking for similarities and differences in relation to appearance and character.

- Pick out three adjectives that most appropriately describe the characters of Manyara and Nyasha. Compare and discuss choices.

2. *Objectives*

- To develop an understanding of the adjective/noun link.

Procedure

- Make individual cards for the following nouns and adjectives which appear in the text. Find appropriate adjectives to describe the noun.

Noun	Adjective
boy	silly
village	rushing
King	finest
snake	worthy
woman	great
water	bad
garments	hungry
daughters	little

- In pairs children make additional adjective cards and then swap with another pair.

3. *Objective*

- To develop understanding of the function and place of commas.

Procedure

- Write out a passage for shared reading without commas. Reread, putting commas in the appropriate places, e.g.

  Arm in arm Nyasha and her father descended the hill crossed the river and approached the city gate. Just as they entered through the great doors the air was rent by piercing cries and Manyara ran wildly out of the chamber at the centre of the enclosure.

- Discuss how commas help with reading and understanding.

Word level work

Objective

- To investigate the relationship between root words and the suffix -ly.

Procedure

- Using words from the adjective list describing Nyasha and Manyara, complete grid and then generate new examples.

root	_____ly
clever strong beautiful sad weak	cleverly

- Model sentence composition with the children using words with -ly suffix.
- Discuss how the words are used.
- Children compose own sentences related to the story.

Jack and the Beanstalk in *British Folk Tales*, by Kevin Crossley-Holland

Jack and the Beanstalk has been known in Britain since the early eighteeth century and probably before. There are many retellings of this traditional folk tale, offering ideal scope for exploration and comparison. Some editors refer to it as a *fairy tale*; the terms *folk tale* and *fairy tale* are interchangeable. Lists of some versions currently available and texts which make reference to the tale are included at the end of this chapter.

At narrative level, the plot of *Jack and the Beanstalk* is a simple one; Jack's well-documented exploits leading him eventually to wealth and happiness. At a symbolic level however, his journey up the beanstalk may represent growing up, escape from domination by his mother to a situation in which he takes control and avenges the death of his father. His actions raise serious moral questions, albeit in a context firmly distanced from reality.

Most of the activities can be adapted for use with other versions of *Jack and the Beanstalk*, but the Crossley-Holland version has been chosen for the richness and beauty of the text, which embodies strong use of figurative language. Enticing words are used to great effect, offering excellent scope for vocabulary extension. The Giant's wife, for example, is described as a 'whey-faced woman'. It would be helpful to establish the meaning of 'whey'* in order that the image can be fully appreciated. Pupils may well be reminded of *Little Miss Muffet*, a nursery rhyme in which the word is used. The ability to make intertextual connections of this kind is an important part of learning to read.

Whey is a bi-product of cheese production and is used extensively in food manufacture. As a homework activity, children could investigate packaging to find foods in which it is an ingredient. This will help to develop *scanning* skills (Reading Comprehension).

* The term chosen for study of this text is Year 5, Term 2 (*See Grid M*).

Grid M *Jack and the Beanstalk* in *British Folk Tales* by K. Crossley-Holland

Year 5 Term 2

Text level	NLS para.	Sentence level	NLS para.	Word level	NLS para.
Reading comprehension • Compile class chart, comparing different versions of the tale	2	**Grammatical awareness** • Investigation of Jack's actions, as indicated by verbs in the text of which he is the subject – drawing attention to the tense used*	2	**Spelling strategies** • Investigation of adjectives in text ending in -ous/-ious*	3
• Construct flowchart of main plot events – transfer to cards, as basis for oral storytelling*	2, 14	• Collection of speech verbs used in this text and others – drawing attention to verb position*	2	• Form adjectives from nouns, using the suffixes -ous/-ious*	3
• Character studies, based on evidence from the text*	8	**Sentence construction and punctuation**		**Spelling conventions and rules** • Collection/investigation of homophones in the text and beyond*	6
• Retelling the story, or parts of it, from a different viewpoint, e.g. that of the giant's wife*	8	• Shared/guided reading, drawing attention to punctuation used in dialogue*	6	**Vocabulary extension** • Collection of metaphorical expressions/figures of speech used in everyday life*	12
• Extract examples of metaphorical language in the text – discuss the images created*	10	• Using cards – match dialogue (direct speech) with reporting clause*	6		
• Think of adjectives to describe the beanstalk – expand into similes*	10	• Invention of further dialogue between e.g. Jack and Martha*	6		
Writing composition • Write alternative versions of the tale, where different decisions alter subsequent events	11				

Text level work

1. Objectives

● To develop literal understanding of plot.
● To develop skills of oral storytelling.

Procedure

● Through discussion, negotiate a flow chart of the main plot events. (Refer to last term's work on text mapping), e.g.

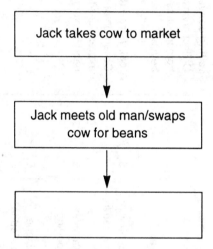

● Children could now retell the tale orally, the events in each box being narrated by different pupils in rotation.

2. Objectives

● To investigate the treatment of different characters in the text.
● To consider alternative narrative viewpoints.
● To develop use/understanding of first person narrative.

Procedure

● Character studies – based on evidence from the text.

   Discuss the characters in the tale. Explore the ways in which we learn about characters e.g. through what they do, what they say, what is said about them.

● Select a character on whom to focus. Ask pupils to suggest words which describe the character; write these on board, flip chart or OHT. Encourage pupils to support their views with evidence from the text.

● Who is narrating the tale? How might events within the tale be narrated from different viewpoints, e.g. that of the giant's wife? Choose an incident to retell in writing from the point of view of a main or peripheral character, using first person narrative mode.

3. Objective

● To develop understanding of differences between literal and figurative language.

Procedure

● During shared/guided reading, discuss the choice of words and the images that are created by them. Particular examples could be used to raise awareness of the difference between literal and figurative language, e.g.

'Then night drew its shutters over the sky and, quite sick with hunger, both she and Jack fell asleep.' (p. 120)
'The sun and the moon looked down on the little smiling cottage at the foot of the beanstalk.' (p. 126)
'The beanstalk had taken root in Jack's mind and it grew from day to day.' (p. 129)
'a huddle of cottages in a cradle of land.' (p. 118)

● Ask: What pictures/images are created in your mind? Which words or phrases particularly interest or puzzle you? Why do you think they were chosen?
● Compare the following sentences from the text:

'Some of the rainbow-beans *had taken root*. Overnight they had sprouted.' (p. 120)
'The beanstalk *had taken root* in Jack's mind and it grew from day to day.' (p. 129)

Key teaching point: The first example uses the concept of 'taking root' literally, while the second uses it figuratively.

4. Objective

● To develop understanding of simile – an aspect of figurative language.

Procedure

● Read aloud:
'Some of the rainbow beans had taken root. Overnight they had sprouted. Their stalks were *thick as slender silver birches*, and as they had spiralled towards the sun, they had entwined *like bindweed*.' p. 120

In this extract, the writer is creating images by using comparison, i.e. he is using *similes*. *Similes* are usually marked by the words 'as' or 'like'.

● Collect examples of similes over time. Some of these will be found in everyday use, e.g. as bold as brass, as white as snow. Compile a class book of similes.

5. Objective

● To encourage the use of similes.

Procedure

● Ask the children to think of adjectives to describe the beanstalk. They should then choose some of the adjectives to develop into similes, e.g.

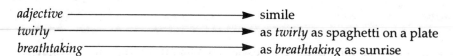

adjective ⟶ simile
twirly ⟶ as *twirly* as spaghetti on a plate
breathtaking ⟶ as *breathtaking* as sunrise

Favourite similes can be written on paper leaves and used to form a class beanstalk.

Sentence level work

1. Objective

● To consolidate recognition of verbs and use of the past tense.

Procedure

● On strips of card, write out some sentences from the text which narrate Jack's actions, e.g.

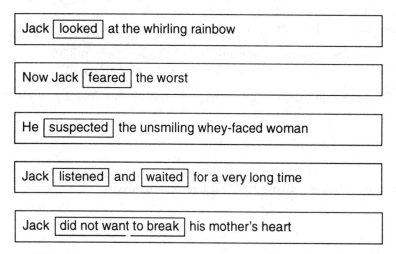

Jack | looked | at the whirling rainbow

Now Jack | feared | the worst

He | suspected | the unsmiling whey-faced woman

Jack | listened | and | waited | for a very long time

Jack | did not want to break | his mother's heart

Highlight the verbs by using a different colour, or perhaps underlining them. Discuss the significance of the highlighted words; reinforce the perception of these words as *verbs*; discuss the *tense* in which they appear and look for *patterns* of past tense formation.

● The children should now gather sentences which narrate the actions of other characters in the story. The *verbs* should be highlighted in some way.

From these verbs, what can be learned about the characters, i.e. their *subjects*.
This will directly link with text level work on Reading Comprehension.

2. Objective

● To show how different verbs can be used to avoid repetition (also Word Level Work).

Procedure

- During shared/guided reading, draw attention to the range of speech verbs used in reporting clauses. Discuss how these indicate the manner in which words were spoken, e.g.

  'There's nothing for supper,' Martha *sobbed* (p. 119)
  'What about you?' *asked* the farmer (p. 119)
  'To have come all this way,' *grumbled* Jack (p. 121)
  'Where is the giant?' *growled* Jack (p. 122)
  'People!' *exclaimed* Jack (p. 123)
  'Am I?' *said* Jack. (p. 123)

3. Objectives

- To revise/reinforce conventions of speech punctuation.
- To develop understanding of how punctuation is the written equivalent of intonation, pauses and gesture.

Procedure

- During shared/guided reading, draw attention to speech punctuation, including the use of question and exclamation marks. (Page 119 in the Crossley-Holland version provides an ideal basis for this discussion.)
- Using prepared cards, children should work in pairs to match dialogue (direct speech) with the reporting clause, e.g.

'Who are these children?'	cried Jack

- Children should now invent and write further dialogue between any two characters at a particular point in the story.

Word level work

1. Objectives

- To develop knowledge of word structure by considering the suffix -ous/-ious, its meaning and grammatical function.
- To show how the suffix can be used to build words from other words.

Procedure 1a.

- Draw attention to words in the text ending in -ous or -ious. Have these words on cards and encourage discussion of the spelling pattern.

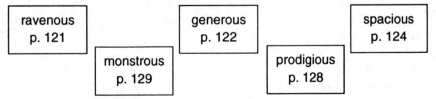

ravenous p. 121

monstrous p. 129

generous p. 122

prodigious p. 128

spacious p. 124

- Discuss the meaning of each word – use dictionaries where appropriate. Note the fact that they are all *adjectives* and identify the *noun* which they describe. For example, *Jack* is described as *ravenous*.

Procedure 1b.

- On another set of cards, write the words from which the above adjectives have been formed or which have the same root or derivation, i.e. raven, generosity, space, monster, prodigy.
- Ask the children to arrange the words in related pairs.

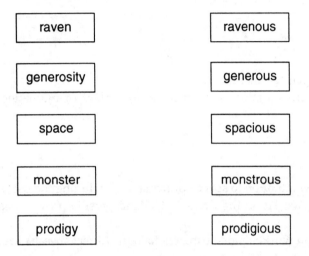

raven	ravenous
generosity	generous
space	spacious
monster	monstrous
prodigy	prodigious

(N.B. Introduce the idea that -ous/-ious is an adjective-forming suffix, meaning 'abounding in', 'characterised by' or 'like'.)

Procedure 1c.

- The children should now form adjectives from the following nouns by the addition of -ous or -ious. Dictionaries should be used.

Noun	Adjective
fame	
joy	
poison	
mountain	
hazard	
curiosity	
envy	
variety	
glory	
religion	
More could be added by the children	

2. Objective

● To revise/develop knowledge of homophones.

Procedure

● During shared/guided reading, attention should be drawn to homophones in the text. (These are words which sound the same but have different meanings and spellings.) e.g. son/sun, meat/meet, right/write, hour/our, grate/great.
● Write homophones on cards; place the cards face down on the table. Include homophones on which you particularly wish to focus; this may vary between groups. In pairs or individually, the children should pick a card, use a dictionary to check its meaning and then compose a sentence which includes it. The card should then be returned *and another one taken*.

3. Objective

● To investigate the use of figurative expressions in everyday life. (This activity is ideal for homework.)

Ask the children to collect expressions which are not used literally. These could be collected over a week or more and added to a class 'bank'. The metaphorical use of 'bank' could itself be discussed. It may be helpful to take a thematic approach, possibly linked to current topics in other curriculum areas, e.g. wood/trees: see Figure 3.6. The 'bank' could take the form of leaves mounted in a wall display.

Figure 3.6

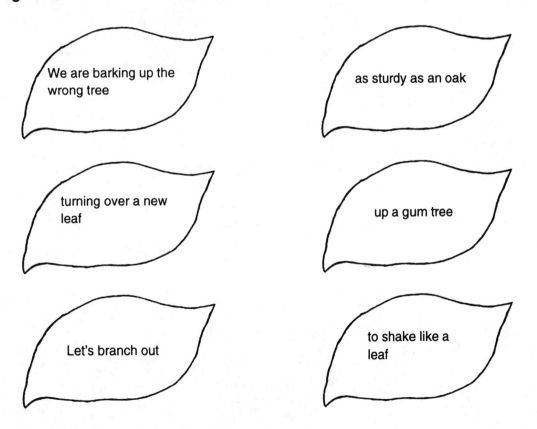

We are barking up the wrong tree

as sturdy as an oak

turning over a new leaf

up a gum tree

Let's branch out

to shake like a leaf

- Introduce *ABC and Things* by Colin McNaughton; in this book, figurative expressions in everyday use are taken literally!

Collections / retellings of Jack and the Beanstalk

E. Ardizzone	(1980)	*English Fairy Tales*
R. Briggs	(1974)	*The Fairy Tale Treasury*
K. Crossley-Holland	(1987)	*British Folk Tales*
A. Daley	(1994)	*Jack and the Beanstalk*
A. Garner	(1993)	*Jack and the Beanstalk*
J. Howe	(1989)	*Jack and the Beanstalk*
R. Impey and I. Beck	(1992)	*Orchard Book or Fairy Tales*
N. Philip	(1992)	*Penguin Book of English Folktales*
T. Ross	(1980)	*Jack and the Beanstalk*

Texts which make reference to the tale:

J. and A. Ahlberg	(1986)	*The Jolly Postman*
R. Briggs	(1973)	*Jim and the Beanstalk*
N. Butterworth	(1992)	*Jasper's Beanstalk*
R. Dahl	(1984)	*Revolting Rhymes*
W. de la Mare	(1947)	*Collected Stories for Children (Dick and the Beanstalk)*
G. Oakley	(1990)	*Once Upon a Time*
M. Waddell	(1990)	*Class Three and the Beanstalk*
B. Wildsmith	(1994)	*Jack and the Meanstalk*

4 Poetry at Key Stages 1 and 2

This chapter looks at one rhyming text and four poems:

Goodnight, Goodnight by Brenda Parkes
If Only I could Take Home a Snowflake by John Agard
The Adventures of Isabel by Ogden Nash
Children Lost by Max Fatchen
The Highwayman by Alfred Noyes.

In our introduction to the Process Model (Chapter 1), we discussed how, in any interaction with texts, we are developing children's creative responses. In the context of poetry, teacher confidence in such development is probably quite low. We intend to provide a supportive framework within which that confidence can grow.

From their earliest experiences of language children develop an awareness of rhythm and rhyme. Through nursery rhymes and playground rhymes they encounter repetition of the patterns of language and further exploration of word play. In teaching poetry, we are building on their inbuilt attraction to words in these ways and although the teaching of poetry is developmental, the principles outlined here apply at all stages.

Benton and Fox (1985) suggest that we move around a poem, viewing it as a sculpture. Our viewpoint helps us to make a part of the meaning; we then need to move and see a different perspective. Readers will then come to know that poetry is about using language in a very precise way. It is about playing with language and images. There is a close 'matching of words with things' (Benton and Fox 1985, p. 21). This is why we focus our attention in 'Children Lost' and 'The Highwayman' on the language and linguistic choices. Poetry makes music with words; makes us look again at familiar things and beyond the familiar to something we might not otherwise notice. Poetry is, therefore, also concerned with keen observation. We stand with the child at the window in John Agard's poem; with Bess as she watches for the Highwayman, or on the moonlit beach in 'Children Lost'.

In extending children's knowledge of form we have chosen a range from simple rhyming text to narrative poetry. Reading aloud these poems will emphasise to children the significance of the form in relation to the subject matter. The galloping rhythm of 'the highwayman's arrival; the breathless anticipation of his return; the sibilant 's' sounds of the sleeping ship and its sad story in 'Children Lost'; these combined with repetition, and line length contribute to the overall effect.

We have also allowed for children to experience the interrelationship between thought and emotion which is concerned with feeling. Writers and readers bring their particular perspectives and reflections to the poem. As readers, we become aware of the writer's feelings, while experiencing our own towards the soldiers or Tim, for example, in 'The Highwayman'; and for the children allowed one night of freedom from the sea in 'Children Lost'.

Although we have suggested a range of activities, they should be introduced sparingly. Children should be encouraged to respond to the parts that interest them, slowly building up a picture of the whole through shared and individual responses. In developing confidence to teach the elements of poetry outlined above, Benton and Fox suggest some general questions which, modified for particular groups, provide an appropriate starting point and have been observed to be of great help.

Language

● Which words, phrases or lines stood out – for whatever reason – when you were reading or listening?

Form

● Can you say anything about the shape of the poem and how the words are laid out on the page?
● Did you notice any patterns?

Observation

● What is the writer really looking at, either outside or inside himself?

Feeling

● What feelings are conveyed during the poem at different points?
● Do they change?
● Do you share them? (p. 21)

The introduction of the NLS provides a much needed framework for progression in the range and type of poetry to introduce to children. We have not focused on writing poetry, as the success of this will depend on the quality of the work carried out at shared and guided reading times. Much support, however, can be gained from Sandy Brownjohn's books *'Does it have to Rhyme?'*, *'What Rhymes with 'Secret'?'*, and *'The Ability to Name Cats'*, and also *'In Tune with Yourself?'* by Jennifer Dunne, Nick Warburton and Morag Styles.

In the first part of this chapter we expand on the importance of phonological awareness through the use of rhyming texts, before looking in more depth at poetry for Key Stages 1 and 2.

Phonological awareness

There is a considerable body of research which demonstrates the importance of a knowledge and understanding of rhyme in the language development of all children. Bryant and Bradley (1985) and Goswami and Bryant (1990) have shown that this knowledge is particularly important in developing phonological awareness. All parents, carers and teachers of young children will have favourite rhymes which they have always shared with children and it is important to remember that these rhymes can still form a significant part of the poetry experiences which are planned for the Literacy Hour.

Sharing poems and rhymes with children helps them to develop pleasure in the sound of words and an implicit knowledge of the ways in which language can be used. Children need to hear and participate in rhyme on a daily basis. Key Stage 1 teachers have always used a range of familiar rhymes regularly to teach an awareness of rhyme as well as for enjoyment. Familiar classroom activities such as finding the days of the week, taking the register and celebrating birthdays can also be used by the teacher as listening activities, which form part of the development of phonological awareness. But some children need more than this. They find reading difficult because they have not developed the ability to make aural discrimination. The ability to hear sounds and rhymes is the first aspect of knowledge about language which children must be taught in Nursery and Reception. Once children have learnt to distinguish sounds, the sounds can be related to the print.

Activities to develop early phonological awareness

- Make sure that 'big book' or poster versions of favourite rhymes are available. Poster versions can be made, laminated and used as a classroom resource.
- Using a wipe-off pen, highlight with the children the words which rhyme.
- Highlight the words which rhyme by sound but not by the appearance of the word. Children need to see spoken language represented in print; in this way they can also begin to understand more about the nature of writing.
- Play games with names to highlight alliteration. Children can make up names for characters or experiment with their own names for example, Pretty Preston and Roaring Rory.
- Children might learn tongue twisters and make up their own.
- Play the 'Odd One Out' game in which the teacher says three words and the children have to find the odd one. In this game, the focus might be initial phonemes (hat, house, garden); ending sounds (jumped, walked, hopping) or middle sounds (feet, seat, book).

These activities form a bridge between raising the children's awareness of literacy, and beginning to develop and extend children's knowledge of phonological awareness. However, children will need more focused and structured teaching if they are to demonstrate a confident knowledge of letter–sound associations. Poetry can be particularly useful in this because of its lively, predictable and often amusing construction. Throughout the NLS document, poetry forms a part of range together with stories, and specific types of poetry are specified for particular terms. We have provided some suggestions for teaching built on specific texts throughout the primary school.

A wide range of books is available to assist you in choosing the type of material that will best suit your teaching objectives and the needs and interests of the children. Some of the most useful are listed below:

J. Agard and G. Nichols, *No Hickory No Dickory No Dock*.
F. Charles, *The Kiskadee Queen*.
D. Gadsby and B. Harrop (eds), *Harlequin*.
B. Harrop, *Okki-Tokki-Unga*.
E. Matterson, *This Little Puffin*.

I. and P. Opie, *The Lore and Language of School Children*.
M. Rosen, *Walking the Bridge of Your Nose*.
C. Sansom, *Speech Rhymes*.

Goodnight, Goodnight by Brenda Parkes, illustrated by Terry Denton

This is a lively, amusing, rhyming text, which utilises both the format of the picture book and also some poetic conventions, with the use of rhyming couplets which are repeated through the text and which invite audience participation. The narrative structure of the text centres on the world of a child falling asleep at night when she is visited by her favourite storybook characters. Although the text indicates that this is a fantasy world 'as we dream the night away', the links between fantasy and reality are blurred, and the element of surprise which surfaces throughout the text suggests opportunities for choice and change as the narrative progresses. The visiting storybook characters, and their overt involvement in the narrative, provide the text with a strong intertextuality which the teacher can exploit in order to emphasise to the children the range of story knowledge which they already possess. The story is told through a first person narrative in the present tense. The use of rhyme provides pace and momentum through the text, and reinforces prediction skills, emphasised through the use of questions addressed directly to the reader, e.g. 'who's that climbing up the stairs?' and 'who's that running as fast as he can?' which produce an instant and enthusiastic response from children.

Similarly, the use of repetition and a repetitive refrain, such as 'Jump on my bed and join the fun . . . There's lots of room for everyone', build confidence in reading, as children rehearse the phrases and sentences and increasingly join with the text in shared reading sessions. This is a text which benefits from being read aloud, so that the teacher can exploit the use of intonation and rhyme and rhythm when reading, emphasising meaning at whole-text level but also the function and use of punctuation. The text also employs different coloured print for emphasis, which again enables the teacher to use this as a starting point for discussion of this device, as well as others such as speech bubbles, which are also used in the text. Within the NLS structure the text would be suitable for use within the Reception year, where the identified range includes 'poetry and stories with predictable structured and patterned language', but also in Year 1, where texts should include 'stories and poems with familiar, predictable and patterned language'. The rhyme patterns of the language used in *Goodnight, Goodnight* range from simple cvc words, e.g. 'can' and 'man' through to the more complex patterning of words such as 'night', 'light' and 'fright'. Grids N and O indicate the potential of this text for Reception and Year 1 classes.

Rhyming texts such as *Goodnight, Goodnight* are also ideal for use as recorded texts which the teacher can then use for children to listen to at the classroom listening post. Recording the text yourself enables you to reinforce the textual patterning which you have used when reading the text aloud in shared reading, thus enabling children to become more familiar with it. Providing children with an individual copy of the text which they follow as they listen to the reading will also reinforce the connections between the written text and the text when read aloud.

Grid N *Goodnight, Goodnight* by Brenda Parkes, illustrated by Terry Denton Year: Reception

Text level	NLS para.	Sentence level	NLS para.	Word level	NLS para.
Reading **Understanding of print**		**Grammatical awareness**		**Phonological awareness, phonics and spelling**	
• Recognise print through shared reading	1	• Ideal text for prediction – rhyme and rhythm of text encourages children to predict	2	• To understand and be able to rhyme through recognising, exploring and working with rhyming patterns	1
• Use taped version and individual copies of text	1	• Use cloze procedure orally*		• Rhyming games* onset/rimes j/ump j/oin j/ig j/ack	4
Reading comprehension				• High frequency words from reading list	6
• List the characters and the different stories they come from	7			• Phoneme/grapheme correspondence	2
• Identify speech bubbles and coloured print italics and significant parts of text	8				
• Use as a basis for own rhyming text involving different characters	10				

Grid O *Goodnight, Goodnight* by Brenda Parkes, illustrated by Terry Denton

Year 1 Term 3

Text level	NLS para.	Sentence level	NLS para.	Word level	NLS para.
Reading comprehension • Discuss questions relating to other stories included in the text – preferences	10	**Grammatical awareness** • Reading aloud with pace and appropriate expression	3	**Revision and consideration from Key Stage 1** • Focus on 'oo' words, e.g. room; contrast with short 'oo' words e.g. book, look, 'ai' words, e.g. stairs, 'oa' words, e.g. cupboard	1
• Reinforce word level skills through shared reading	1	• Discuss word order, suggest other words which might be substituted – discuss author's choice	4	• 'i.e.' words, e.g. friend • Word recognition etc.	6
• Compare and contrast stories with a variety of settings*	8	• Use cloze procedure		• Investigate and learn spellings of words with 'ing' pattern, e.g. looking, climbing, running	
Writing activities • Write about significant incidents from known stories – write the significant incidents from those stories which form part of the narrative	13	**Sentence construction** • Revise capitalisation (Year 1 Term 2) consider capital letters for names of all characters in text	5	**Handwriting** • Teach patterns to match spelling, e.g. ai, oa (horizontal joins without ascender) • -ing (horizontal joins without descender)	10
		• List names of characters and provide names (with capital letters) for those characters not named in the text*			
		• Remove question marks and ask children to put them in on laminated copy	7		

Text level work

Objectives

- To compare and contrast common themes in stories and poems.
- To emphasis and explore the rhyme of the text and other texts which comprise part of it.

Procedure

- Reread text identifying other stories and rhymes which form an integral part of the text.
- Children work in pairs to retell the story of one of those mentioned in the text, i.e. Goldilocks, Old Mother Hubbard, Jack and the Beanstalk, The Gingerbread Man.
- Alternatively the teacher can choose to focus on one of the texts above and ask children to retell the focused text in six (or eight) pictures each with a sentence.
- Highlight the differences between the prose versions of these retellings and the rhyme of the original.

Sentence level work

1. Cloze procedure

Objectives

- To promote the use of content and meaning in reading.
- To develop prediction skills (focusing on appropriate substitution).

Procedure

- Read the text aloud, pausing at approximately every seventh word and encouraging the children to suggest suitable words to 'fit the gap'.
- If the children find this difficult, repeat the beginning of the phrase or sentence and then read two or three of the words following the 'gap'. This encourages the use of the grammatical structure of the text to aid identification of appropriate individual words.
- Cloze procedure can also be used to focus on particular categories of words, e.g. adjectives or nouns, or parts of words e.g. prefixes or suffixes (which occur later in the teaching schedule). It is important that the teacher does not immediately produce a word which occurs in the original text, as the children need to be encouraged to think about appropriate words and word classes.

2. Capitalisation

This can also be used with question marks and other features of punctuation.

Objective

- To revise the use of capitalisation for names.

Procedure

- Using a laminated text and a highlighter, reread text with children, highlighting all the capital letters used in the text.
- Consider why each capital letter is used.
- On flipchart, list names of characters in text.
- Follow this up by children working individually in a group on a copy of their own in which capital letters have been removed.
- Ask children to change lower case letters into capitals where capital letters are required.

Word level work

1. Word endings

Objective

- To investigate and learn spellings of -ing (present tense).

Procedure

- Reread text with a small group of children.
- Each child has a (laminated) copy of the text.
- Write the ending -ing and ask the children to find it on their copy and to draw a circle round it with a marker pen.

Write out the words from the text which end in -ing and then ask the children to think of others. Make a list of all the words children can remember which end in -ing.

2. Rhyming words

Objective

- To build on children's knowledge of rhyme and rhythm.

Procedure

- Use a set of laminated cards on which you have written all the rhyming words from the text. Using different coloured pens for the 'rime' and 'onset', ask the children to read them with you, matching them to the text. Then, using a board or a flip chart, stick the words on the board in rhyming lists to emphasise the 'rime' of each word.
- Ask children for suggestions of other rhyming words not in the text which could be included in the list.
- This activity can be extended into shared writing activity, where the class make up their own rhymes using the rhyming words.

'The Adventures of Isabel' by Ogden Nash, in *Poems Not to be Missed*

Much of the work with younger children involves using rhyme and texts which utilise a rhyming narrative. 'The Adventures of Isabel' continues this tradition, but offers the opportunity to lead Year 2 children into more sophisticated poetry, as the NLS requires for this age group. The anthology *Poems Not to be Missed* provides an excellent model of what an anthology comprises, and as it is available in a big book version, enables the teacher to clearly specify the characteristics, e.g. categories of poetry, variety of authors, which an anthology contains. Susan Hill's introduction suggests that teachers need to introduce issues such as what poetry comprises, as well as discussing with children the place that poetry has in our lives in terms of our ideas and emotions (p. 4), and our responses to these.

Furthermore, this anthology contains a range of varieties of poetry. These include nonsense poems (Year 2, Term 3): the text is clearly set out with indexes by title, author and first line, thus enabling children to learn to use the contents page and index to find their way about text (Year 2, Term 3).

The poem 'The Adventures of Isabel' falls into general categories under the NLS heading of range; these include 'humorous verse', poems with predictable and patterned language, and poems by significant children's authors. Whether Ogden Nash falls into this category is debatable: he is clearly significant, but whether his verse is intended for children requires debate.

'The Adventures of Isabel' is listed under the category of Play and Nonsense in the text, sandwiched between Hilaire Belloc's 'Cautionary Tales of Matilda' and a bear limerick – and both of these could also be used by the teacher to discuss with children texts which play with language (Year 2, Term 3).

'The Adventures of Isabel' offers opportunities to play with ideas and to challenge ideas and conventions with humour. It is the amusing story in verse of how Isabel copes with a variety of challenges including a bear, (graphically pictured hovering over her with venomous intent), a witch, and a terrifying dream. As Isabel refuses to be cowed by any of these experiences (and others), the poem offers the opportunity to discuss how and why she deals with the situations in the way she does. The symbolism of the poem enables children to face their fears with regard to a world which is bigger and more powerful than they are. Symbolically it offers reassurance that even those who are less powerful can survive and win. There are parallels here with fairy tales and the Bettleheim (1979) hypothesis that such stories offer the opportunity for children to face their fears through fantasy. The humour of the poem results from its nonsensical aspect – Isabel turns the tables on those characters who threaten her very existence by treating them in the way that they wished to treat her. The victim becomes the victor in each of the five verses, all of which contains the same patterning. Isabel meets the character who is described as fearsome, and who then threatens Isabel with a gruesome fate. Isabel, however, refuses on each occasion to be panicked. Having calmly considered the situation, she deals with each protagonist in turn. The final longer verse has a nightmare as its focus, and enables the author to address the reader directly and to exhort courage in the face of challenge and danger.

The text employs ten-line verses with five rhyming couplets in each. Some of the rhymes are half rhymes, e.g. 'horrid' and 'forehead'. The text is repetitive and rhythmic and includes several words which end in the suffix -ly. There are several uses of the vowel phonemes 'or', 'er', 'air' (Year 2, Term 2). Building on this knowledge make this text suitable for use at Year 2, Term 3, as Grid P shows.

The linguistic structure offers a richness at all levels and enables the teacher to revisit and revise work previously undertaken as well as leading into Year 3, Term 1, focusing further on punctuation such as exclamation marks as well as commas.

Apart from the last verse, the poem is written in the past tense. It is only in the final verse, when the author challenges the reader to tackle nightmares as Isabel did, that the present tense is used. Discussion of the choices of tense made by the author could be used to draw attention to the reasons for these differences, and the impact the use of tense has on meaning and structure. Although work on tenses does not feature in the schedule for Year 2, Term 3, it does feature in the subsequent term's work, and for some children it will be appropriate.

Text level work

What makes a nonsense poem?

Objective

● To discuss meanings of words and phrases that create humour in poetry.

Procedure

Reread text in shared reading. Use as a basis for discussion of the patterns and puzzles in the text, e.g.

● How does Isabel manage to eat a bear?
● How, and why does she deal with the doctor in the way that she does?
● What is really happening in the last verse?
● What do we know about Isabel? What kind of person is she?
● Which specific words and/or phrases do we find amusing?
● Why is it a 'nonsense' poem?

Such discussion of the interpretation of the text can also lead into work on character, which is also specified for this term.

Word level work

Finding and using -ly

Objective

● To identify, list and use words ending in the suffix -ly.

Procedure

● Reread text with children using pointer to highlight all words which end in -ly.
● Provide children, in pairs, with a laminated copy of the text. Ask them to circle these words,

Grid P   'The Adventures of Isabel' by Ogden Nash, in *Poems Not To Be Missed*, Susan Hill and Debby Strauss (eds)   Year 2 Term 3

Text level	NLS para.	Sentence level	NLS para.	Word level	NLS para.
Reading comprehension • Ideal text for shared reading • Book talk – response to text • Which words and phrases are funny – why it's nonsense, e.g. Isabel turns the table on all her protagonists	1 6 8	**Grammatical awareness** • Reading aloud with appropriate intonation and expression • Teacher reads aloud and children participate • Retell story of Isabel in prose – orally • Encourage use of standard forms of verbs and past tense consistency	2 1 3	**Phonological awareness, phonics and spelling** • Work on 'ea', e.g. head, bread, are both found in the text, as are dream and bear. Starting point for work on collections of words containing these phonemes	3
Writing composition • Use as a basis for writing own shared version – could be part of work on nonsense poetry	9 11			**Word recognition and graphic knowledge** • Investigating words which have the same spelling patterns but different sounds, e.g. ea words	6
				• Collecting the rhyming words from the text making lists of others words with same rhyme – also words which have same spelling patterns but different sounds	7

				• Looking for suffix '-ly' ugly
				  quietly
				  calmly
				  really
				• Using words in the text as starting points	

				Vocabulary extension • Why did author use specific words, e.g. 'rancour', – what does it mean? What are the alternatives?	9
				• Unusual/new words, e.g. 'zwieback' (a kind of sweet rusk or biscuit) • Why were the witch's gums 'sprinkled' with teeth?	10

and then to write them carefully on separate pieces of card, using different coloured pens for the root of the word and the suffix -ly.

> ugly
> quietly
> calmly
> really

- In their twos, they should identify other words that end in -ly, through the use of other texts in the classroom, including dictionaries and word banks.
- Write these words too on separate pieces of card.
- When they have collected ten words ending in -ly, the words can be displayed on an -ly board, and discussed as part of the plenary session.

'If Only I Could Take Home a Snowflake' by John Agard, illustrated by Suzanna Gretz, from *I Din Do Nuttin and Other Poems*

'If Only I Could Take Home a Snowflake' is one of a collection of poems by Guyanese poet John Agard. The collection is very focused on children's experiences and many of the themes are those common to children everywhere – the purchase of new shoes, the failure to get an answer from parents to questions asked. Other poems in this collection focus specifically on experiences based in Guyana, offering the opportunity for discussion of different cultures, their similarities and differences. 'Three-Hole', about a Guyanese marble game is one such example, as is 'Sugarcane', which focuses on a child's liking for eating sugarcane, and her grandmother's disapproval of her eating it at the same time as trying to do her homework!

'If Only I Could Take Home a Snowflake' is a short poem (as are most in this collection) which centres on a child's view of snowflakes and his wish to take one back to Guyana to show his friends there. The poem consists of four verses, one of which is repeated as the third verse. The language used in this poem is non-standard English. The differences that exist, such as the non-use of a verb in the repeated verse, can be used to discuss the function of verbs, and to consider why the poem still makes sense without one in this verse. There is a limited use of rhyme in the final verse, which ends with 'in the sun' 'just for fun just for fun', and the use of 'rum' and 'come' in verse 2.

The line shape of the poem offers opportunities for discussion, and the repeated verse, which is composed of one powerful simile, could be used as a useful starting point for discussion of similes. As part of a whole-class session, children could brainstorm their own images.

> 'Snowflakes
> like tiny
> insects
> drifting
> down'

The shape of this verse reflects its subject matter, and could also be used to discuss the layout of poems and why the author has chosen a specific format. Furthermore, the author's choice of language can be used as a starting point for work on words and phrases that create impact (Year 3, Term 1) e.g. the use of 'drifting'. The image of snowflakes as 'tiny insects' is extended and developed in the following verse by the phrases:

> 'without a hum
> they come,
> without a hum
> they go'

This clearly identifies the eerie silence which often accompanies snow falling.

Although this is a short poem, some focused work on snow and poems that have snow as their theme could include this one and others on the theme. See for example 'Dust of Snow' by Robert Frost, 'First Snow' by Marie Louise Allen or 'The Snowflake' by Walter de la Mare (all in the *Walker Book of Poetry for Children*, compiled by J. Prelutsky and published in 1983 by Random House). Such comparative work would also lead to discussion about preferences, and the reasons children provide for their views. We have developed our ideas in the context of Year 3, Term 1 as Grid Q indicates.

Text level work

Snow shape poems

Objective

- To develop own shape poems (calligrams) on the theme of snowflakes choosing appropriate vocabulary to convey meaning and image

Procedure:

- Look at the shape (outline) of 'If Only I Could Take Home a Snowflake' and other snow poems.
- Discuss differences in shape, and consider what an appropriate shape for a snowflake poem might be. (Locate information about the shape of snowflakes from information texts.)
- Brainstorm adjectives which suggest snow and snowflakes.)
- Model how these words might be combined to produce an impact on the reader which suggest snow.
- Children to produce their own after participating in the class modelling.

Sentence level work

Snow verbs

Objective

- To understand that verbs can be used to develop writing descriptively and to enhance meaning and image.

Grid Q   'If Only I Could Take Home a Snowflake' by John Agard, illustrated by Suzanna Gretz   Year 3 Term 1

Text level	NLS para.	Sentence level	NLS para.	Word level	NLS para.
Reading comprehension • Read aloud and recite (as part of selection of poems about snowflakes) • Make comparisons between different poems	 6	**Grammatical awareness** • Identify verbs in poems List them and consider why the author has chosen to omit a verb in one sentence and what that verb should be	 3, 4	**Revision and consideration from Key Stage 1** • Identify syllables in words such as 'snowflake' 'insects' 'drifting' 'without'	 4
• Discuss poet's choice of words, e.g. drifting, insects	6	• Change verbs in poem. Discuss alternatives and their impact on the poem	3, 4	**Spelling strategies** • List words which can be spelt by analogy with 'snow', e.g. throw, tow, bow, crow, show, now, brow, grow • Discuss homonyms and homophones	 6
• Consider rhyme and non-rhyming sections and layout	7	• List verbs which could be used about snow*	3, 4		
• Discuss children's view of the poem why does one child in the poem want to take a snowflake home? Where is home? How do you know? Why does the poet use the simile 'like tiny insects'?	8	**Sentence construction and punctuation** • Present poem as spoken language either in speech bubbles or through the use of speech marks • Include capitalisation appropriately	 7, 8, 9		
Writing comprehension • Draw shape of poem • Discuss and compare with shapes of other snowflake poems*	13				
Non-fiction • Find information about snow through information retrieval devices • Compare fact and fiction	16				

Procedure

- Identify the verbs in the poem by highlighting them on a copy of the text – then compare with the verbs in other snow poems which authors have used to describe the movement of snow.
- List other verbs which could be used descriptively about snow.
- This activity can also be used as an alphabetic activity, reinforcing alphabetic knowledge by suggesting a verb relating to snow for each letter of the alphabet, e.g.

  snow arrives
  snow bathes
  snow cascades
  snow drives
  snow escapes
  snow falls

- For children who find it difficult to identify which word is a verb, simplify this activity by writing a range of verbs on cards, some of which would be unlikely to be used descriptively about snow. Get children to sort out through discussion which verbs they would use when writing about snow and which they would not. The chosen verbs can be used as a starting point for the children's own snow poem.

'Children Lost' by Max Fatchen, in *Poems Not to be Missed*

This descriptive poem recounts a mysterious event: the appearance of a wreck and its associated story. The impact of the poem lies in its powerful use of imagery, personification and alliteration. Children are fascinated by the mystery surrounding the wreck and the events of the fateful night. The poem offers the opportunity for detailed study of expressive and descriptive language, and writing activities supported by the ideas and events described. The work outlined is set in the context of Year 4, Term 2, (see Grid R).

Text level

1. Objectives

- To understand how mood is created through the use of expressive language.
- To appreciate the picture that the poet is attempting to create.

Procedure

Shared reading
- Teacher reads and rereads the poem, children listen and follow. Expression and intonation will be an essential feature of the teacher's reading.
- Children discuss what type of poem this is in relation to mood. It recounts a tale and seeks to explain why the ship was wrecked. It is mysterious, sad, ghostly.
- Children read the poem/ballad with the teacher attempting to capture that mood.

71

Grid R   'Children Lost' by Max Fatchen, in *Poems Not To Be Missed*, Susan Hill and Debby Strauss (eds)   Year 4 Term 2

Text level	NLS para.	Sentence level	NLS para.	Word level	NLS para.
Reading comprehension • Explore the use of expressive and descriptive language in recreation of mood and emotion*	4	**Grammatical awareness** • Extend work on adjectival phrases*	1	**Revision from Year 3** • Revise knowledge of phonemes/syllables and syllabic patterns*	11, 12
• Identify and discuss aspects of figurative language, e.g. personification, imagery*	5	**Sentence construction and punctuation** • Extend work on the apostrophe for both contraction and possession. Include both singular and plural nouns*	2	**Vocabulary extension** • Explore context specific words, e.g. hands, ribs and define succinctly*	
• Investigate the rhyming pattern and verse structure and read aloud effectively*	7	• Consider word order in relation to rhythm, repetition and use of questions			
Writing composition • Write own piece of descriptive language as a newspaper report of the actual event*	13				

- As the week progresses different 'readings' can be explored, e.g. choral speaking, taped versions.

Guided / independent activities at text level
Groups of children can focus on the following aspects:

- finding words that contribute to the mood of the poem, e.g. lonely, wild (cliffs), moonlit, cold;
- finding words and phrases that are associated with the ghostly themes, e.g. ghostly beach, cold-eyed moon, figures, haunted.

2. Objective

- To understand the use of personification in the poem.

Procedure

This technique is best introduced during shared reading and can then be developed by children working in groups, following the teacher's directions.

- Finding words and phrases where the author has used language to describe the elements that relate to human actions and emotion.

Wind	Sea
sly winds	cunning sea
	eager waves' wild roar
	selfish sea
voice of wind	(voice of) tide

- Children could then add to the list with their own suggestions,
  e.g. wicked winds; thoughtless sea

3. Objective

- To understand the rhyming pattern of the poem and its verse structure.

Procedure

- shared reading discussion should focus on the ABCB pattern and the occasional use of ternal rhyme. e.g. crew . . . threw (verse 7). Group work can then focus on children aking and sorting lists. This work will also develop word work on syllabic pattern.
- list of rhyming word pairs can be gathered,

e.g.	sides	tides
	blew	too
	steep	sleep
	wreck	deck
	roar	ashore
	stone	own

and then sorted into pairs which have the same rime,

| i.e. | sides | tides | – the same letter string after the onset |

and those which rhyme but do not have the same letter string

i.e.	blew	too
	roar	ashore
	there	air

This work is particularly important for inexperienced readers and can be linked to handwriting and spelling strategy work.

4. Writing composition

Objective

• To develop use of descriptive language in a shared context.

Procedure

• Create a fact list about: the ship; the weather at the time of the loss; the people on board.
• Write a newspaper report as a reporter working for the South Australian Post. You are asked to write a report about the shipwreck of 'The Ethel', a sailing boat bringing immigrants from England in 1880. There are no survivors; all lives were lost at sea.
• Prompts should encourage children to include:

    – details of the vessel, its journey, age etc;
    – the weather at the time of the shipwreck;
    – the warning of local people;
    – the reason why the ship was close to the reef;
    – what people saw that night and the next morning.

Sentence level

1. Objectives

• To revise/introduce work on adjectives used to describe key nouns.
• To explore what happens when word order is changed.

Procedure

• Children in groups take different nouns from the text, given by the teacher, and create spider diagrams of words used to describe them. Ideas can be given and below are some completed examples:

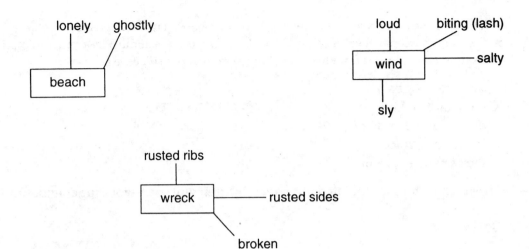

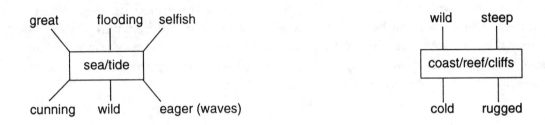

- Make suggestions as to why the poet chooses these adjectives.
- Link to text level work to discuss in shared sessions:
  - How/when is the sea cunning/selfish/eager?
  - What do we know about the ship's structure?

2. Sentence construction and punctuation

Objectives

- To identify the use of the possessive apostrophe in reading the poem.
- To consider the apostrophe used for contractions.

Procedure

- Clearly this text offers the opportunity for work on the apostrophe in all the examples given in Objective 2 at 'sentence level work'.

Possession		Contraction
Singular Noun	**Plural Noun**	
Sailor's boast	Waves' wild roar	It's We'll
Reef's cold rock		He's
Dolphin's track		
(N.B. 'its own')		

- At the earliest point of understanding, awareness should be heightened. This is best done in focused word and sentence work.

75

- It needs to be a key objective for one or two days, not discussed in passing.
- The children could then revise and practise their understanding in a range of activities, creating noun phrases from the poem but using their own ideas, e.g.

> the wreck's ribs
> the wind's whine
> the children's mothers
> the sailors' voices
> the sea kings' promise

These can be teacher-initiated but some children will soon work independently.

Contractions

These appear widely in conversation/dialogue and awareness of them is heightened through regular discussion and practice. A dialogue between the children and the sea kings or the poet and friend could be role-played and scripted by the teacher or children. Demonstration by the teacher is essential, but children will always find unusual examples, so be prepared for the unexpected use of the apostrophe. Regular and systematic revision throughout the term, using the apostrophe in a shared context, is far more successful than endless exercises.

Word level work

1. Objectives

- To reinforce knowledge of syllables and syllabic pattern.
- To understand links between rhyming words at syllabic level.

Procedure

- Activities to reinforce the above include counting and recording syllables finding two syllable words.
- Compare words such as:

rusted		wrecked
rugged	*with*	hauled
haunted		dreamed
		drowned

2. Vocabulary extension

Objectives

- To explore words with other meanings in a context.
- To define different meanings in four, three, two, one word(s).

Procedure

- Use dictionaries to collect a range of meanings for:

ribs	bond
hands	bound
form	figures
drive	

- Devise quiz games where definitions only are given.

The Highwayman by Alfred Noyes, illustrated by Charles Keeping

This powerful narrative poem can be found in several anthologies. This version is illustrated by Charles Keeping and has particular impact because of the black and white illustrations and the interpretation they offer. This, of course, would be an excellent point for discussion. Noyes wrote the poem in 1913, Keeping illustrated it in 1981. Although Grid S focuses on Term 2 of Years 5 and 6, clearly this poem could also be introduced in Term 1 of Year 5 and act as a starting point for work in Term 2.

What does this text teach?

- It is a narrative poem with strong imagery developed through both metaphor and simile.
- At a symbolic level it explores the themes of love, bravery, sacrifice and other moral dilemmas.
- Both inference and deduction can be developed through study of the text. Certain things are implied and can be inferred, e.g. the role of Tim.
- It is a third person narrative – but the story is very much told from a particular viewpoint.
- Historical context and vocabulary can be developed.
- There is repetition of language within a repeated structure.
- Rhythm is linked to the subject matter.
- Tense changes with time passing – i.e. from past to ongoing/continuous present.
- Alliteration is an aspect of the figurative language.

The text would also be enhanced by a performance.

Text level work

1. Objectives

- To develop understanding of narrative structure.
- To map the passage of time through the poem.

Procedure

- On reading and rereading the poem, track the time sequence to answer the question: 'How long does the story take to happen?'

Grid S *The Highwayman* by Alfred Noyes, illustrated by Charles Keeping   Year 5/6 Term 2

Text level	NLS para.	Sentence level	NLS para.	Word level	NLS para.
Reading comprehension • Use discussion framework, e.g. 'Tell Me' (Chambers). Consider the story in a time sequence and explore its narrative structure*	Y5: 4, 6 Y6: 1	**Grammatical awareness** • Consider the effect of changing word order in the introduction on meaning and rhythm*	Y5: 1	**Spelling conventions and rules** • Investigate verbs that have -ed or -ing added and form hypotheses*	Y5: 4
• Explore use of language to highlight the treatment of different characters*	Y5: 8	• Look at the effect of tense change between the beginning and the end on verbs and verb endings*	Y5: 2	**Vocabulary extension** • Investigate unusual context – specific words, e.g. 'rapier', 'harry', 'stable-wicket' and create glossary – link to history topic if appropriate	Y5: 9
• Investigate figurative language and its effects* • Explore rhythm, rhyme and repetition with the text*	Y5: 10 Y6: 5 Y6: 3	**Sentence construction and punctuation** • Investigate the conditional 'if they ...' and its significance for the plot	Y6: 5	• Consider onomatopoeia 'tlot-tolt' and the gallop-like rhythm of the poem	Y5: 11
• Evaluate the poem and its impact	Y6: 6, 8	• Compare simple and compound sentences with complex sentences used in stories*	Y6: 3 Y5: 8		
Writing composition • Write version of story through other characters' eyes using flashbacks • Write alternative metaphors and similes linked to the text	Y6: 11 Y5: 12				

Day	Time	Main event
Day One	Late	Bess and Highwayman meet
Day Two	Sunset	King George's men arrive
Day Two	Midnight	Bess kills herself
Day Three	Noon	Highwayman is killed
'Today'		Bess and Highwayman meet

- The class, as a whole or in groups, can make a list in order of the time markers that indicate the passing of time.
- An oral retelling will help some children to reinforce this important concept. See the 'Hold Them in your Hand' activity for *Mr Gumpy's Motor Car*.

2. Objective

- To develop an understanding of narrative viewpoint through an exploration of the language used in the treatment of different characters.

Procedure

- Using copies of the poem, groups track the actions of one of these four characters:

Bess	Highwayman
soldiers	Tim

- The children discuss and make notes on how the verbs tell us about the characters, their motives and behaviour.
- They create questions for other groups to consider in order to build up views and opinions. Teacher prompts may be needed in the early stages, e.g. the Highwayman's actions are not related to robbing and stealing, other than by inference. Why might this be? There are no action verbs associated with Tim. Does he act? Why is he a character? What are our feelings towards the soldiers? How is this achieved?
- In addition, one could expand the 'Tell Me' (Chambers 1994) framework to consider puzzles such as what the landlord was doing/saying while the soldiers used his daughter as a bait? What did Tim hope would happen?

The actions of characters in the poem

Highwayman	*Tim*
riding	listened
clattered	loved
clashed	heard
tapped his whip on the shutters	
whistled a tune to the window	
rose upright	
face burnt like a brand	
kissed	
tugged his rein	
galloped away	
turned	
spurred to the west	
shouted	

Bess	*soldiers*
plaited a dark-red love knot	marched
loosened her hair	drank
twisted her hands	gagged
writhed her hands	bound
stretched and strained	knelt with muskets
strove no more	tied her up
would not risk their hearing	sniggered
stood up straight and still	bound a musket beside her
her eyes grew wide	kissed her
took one last deep breath	looked to their priming
warned him with her death	shot him down
watched for her love	
died in the darkness	

3. Objectives

● To develop an understanding of figurative language and its effects.

Several activities will be outlined here. It will be for the teacher to decide whether they form part of the shared reading session or group activities. This decision will be made with the children's previous experience and levels of understanding in mind.

Procedure

● Using the list or part of the list, children with or without the teacher sort similes and metaphors and group them under headings where appropriate, e.g.

road	*Tim*
ribbon of moonlight	hollows of madness (eyes)

● Consider the effect of these images and the pictures they create. How has Charles Keeping shown this? Do we agree with his interpretation?
● Children write their own metaphors and similes as alternatives.

Metaphor M Simile S Onomatopoeia O

torrent of darkness (wind)	M
ghostly galleon (moon)	M
jewelled sky	M
hollows of madness (Tim's eyes)	M
hair like mouldy hay (Tim)	S
burnt like a brand (face)	S
black cascade of perfume (hair)	M
a gypsy's ribbon (road)	M
looping the purple moor (road)	M
the hours crawled by like years	S
blank and bare in the moonlight	M
tlot-tlot in the frosty silence	O/M
tlot-tlot in the echoing night	O/M
her face was like a light (Bess)	S

| her musket shattered the moonlight | M |
| back, he spurred like a madman (Highwayman) | S |

- Children can track the colour red and descriptions of light and dark in preparation for discussion. How does the use of colour create mood and atmosphere? Why does Keeping use black/white?

Red	*Light*	*Dark*
claret velvet (coat)	lace	torrent of darkness (wind)
dark red love knot	jewelled sky	long black hair
red-lipped (Bess)	yellow gold	black eyed
burnt like a brand (face)	morning light	dark old inn-yard
red-coat troop	tawny sunset	hall/death
red blood	golden noon	black cascade
blood-red (spurs)		grey (face)
wine-red (coat)		

- Work on alliteration from Year 3 could be revisited or, in the early stages of the Strategy, be introduced for the first time.

Sentence level work

Objective

- To develop an understanding of the changes to verbs in the past to present shift.

Procedure

- Using the introductory section and the final refrain, the children should make a list of the verbs and note the changes.
- They should note what changes and what does not, and consider why this should be.

Past	*Present*
came	comes
was	is
was locked and barred	is locked and barred
whistled	whistles
should be waiting	should be waiting
plaiting	plaiting

Objective

- To develop knowledge of sentence construction through the comparison of compound and complex sentence.
- To explore with the teacher how the clauses are constructed as compound or simple sentences using character descriptions.

For example: 'He'd . . .
. . . and breeches of brown doe skin'   COMPOUND
'They fitted . . .' }

}——SIMPLE

'His boots . . .' }

- Either in shared writing sessions or as groups, the children could write descriptions in prose that use COMPLEX sentences, e.g. His breeches, which were made from brown doe skin, fitted without a wrinkle. Tim, the ostler, whose face was white and peaked, listened in the dark old inn-yard. His eyes were hollows of madness and his hair was like mouldy hay. What effect does this have on the reader? Is it better? If not, why not? Comparisons with descriptions from novels and short stories could be made and experienced children could work changing prose to poetry and vice-versa.
- Issues of word and clause order, the absence of connectives and the repetition of words can all be discussed in relation to the rhythm and meaning of the poem.

Questions to consider

- Is there pattern to the repetition?
- What effect does phrasing have?

For example: 'Dumb as a dog, he listened . . .'
            rather than
            'He listened, dumb as a dog.'
            'Blood-red were his spurs . . .'
            rather than
            'His spurs were blood-red.'

- What is the rhyme pattern? Does it restrict or enhance the poem?
- What is the rhythmical beat?
- How would we read/perform the poem?

Word level work

Objective

- To develop understanding of the spelling patterns related to verb endings.

Procedure

- During shared reading or writing, attention should be given to the verbs where -ed or -ing have been added and children could then create lists and look for patterns.

toss	tossed	kiss	kissed
fit	fitted	throb	throbbed
whistle	whistled	spur	spurred
clatter	clattered	turn	turned
clash	clashed	ride	riding
creak	creaked	plait	plaiting
tug	tugged	tumble	tumbling
gag	gagged	march	marching
		shout	shouted

- Explore when consonants double, and when 'e' is omitted.
- Create a class grid for children to add to over the term, looking at key points and patterns.

	Root words (double consonant)	Present/ participle (-*ing*)	Past participle (-*ed*)	Simple past (irregular)
double consonant	fit	fitting	fitted	
	hit	hitting		hit
	spur	spurring	spurred	
	occur	occurring	occurred	
no change	clatter	clattering	clattered	
	turn	turning	turned	
	clash	clashing	clashed	
	kiss	kissing	kissed	
dropping 'e'	ride	riding	ridden	rode
	stride	striding		strode
	hide	hiding	hidden	hid
	march	marching	marched	
	shout	shouting	shouted	

This will form the basis of word work and spelling patterns and rules throughout the term.

5 Introducing the novel at Key Stage 2

Novels and stories present many opportunities for activities at all three levels within the NLS Framework. To explore all of them would not be possible or desirable, and one of the most important decisions the teacher will have to make is *which* aspects of the book to focus on in order both to meet NLS objectives *and* develop children's understanding and enjoyment of the text. In addition, time will be needed for the teacher to read the novel and to provide children with opportunities to explore initial responses, before the focused work begins. In this chapter, a short novel is considered and ideas presented which could be adapted for use at different stages of children's development. Three grids are included (Grids T, U and V), indicating where the study of this novel would be appropriate in relation to the requirements on range, and highlighting the relevant objectives. This may be particularly useful where classes include more than one year group. The detailed activities are intended for use in Year 5, Term 1, but many of them could be adapted for use in Year 4.

Charlotte's Web by E. B. White

Charlotte's Web is a familiar, well-loved novel with elements of fantasy and anthropomorphism. It is written in the third person and events are described in chronological order. Factual information about the animals is embedded within the narrative and the author explores facets of human nature through distinctive characterisation. The authenticity of the setting, a farm in rural America, is an important factor in encouraging the reader to suspend disbelief and E. B. White uses both humour and pathos to evoke response. The dramatic nature of the opening and the satisfying sense of closure at the end contribute to the novel's balanced, cyclical structure.

At narrative level, the story is that of a small pig, Wilbur, the runt of his litter, whose life is saved first by Fern, a young girl, and then, more dramatically, by Charlotte, a spider. When Charlotte dies Wilbur takes on the responsibility for her young, an indication of his own growth into maturity. There are strong descriptions of rural life, informed by White's own love of the countryside and of its people and animals.

At a symbolic level the novel explores themes such as friendship; innocence and experience/wisdom; cyclical patterns of life and nature; the relationship between parents and child; and the importance of language and its effects.

One of the most interesting linguistic features of the book is the extensive use of dialogue, including examples of formality. Indeed the book opens with dialogue and the use of a striking lead question: 'Where's Papa going with that axe?' (p. 7) There is

Grid T Range: Fiction and Poetry: short novels

Year 4 Term 1

Text level	NLS para.	Sentence level	NLS para.	Word level	NLS para.
Reading comprehension • Investigate how settings and characters are built up from small details and how the reader responds to them.	1	**Grammatical awareness** • Investigate verb tenses (past, present and future – compare sentences from narrative and information texts. Develop awareness of how tense relates to purpose and structure of text	2	**Revision and consolidation from Year 3** • Read and spell words through: – identifying syllabic patterns in multi-syllabic words	1
• Identify the main characters, drawing on the text to justify views, and using the information to predict actions	2	• Understand the term 'tense' (i.e. that it refers to time) in relation to verbs and use it appropriately		**Spelling strategies** • Use independent spelling strategies, including: – building from other words with similar patterns and meanings – spelling by analogy	3
• Explore chronology in narrative using a written text, by mapping how much time passes in the course of the story	3	• Identify the use of powerful verbs, e.g. 'hobbled' instead of 'went'	3	• Spell regular verb endings • Spell irregular tense changes (link these with sentence level work)	7 8
• To explore narrative order: introductions → build-ups → climaxes or conflicts → resolutions	4	• Identify adverbs and understand their function in sentences through: – identifying common adverbs with -ly suffix and discussing their impact on the meaning of sentences – noticing where they occur in sentences and how they are used to qualify the meaning of verbs	4	**Vocabulary extension** • Define familiar vocabulary in their own words, using alternative phrases or expressions	11
Writing composition • Plan a story identifying the stages of its telling	10				
• Write character sketches, focusing on small details to evoke sympathy or dislike	11				

Grid U   Range: Fiction and Poetry: stories/novels about imagined words: fantasy   Year 4 Term 2

Text level	NLS para.	Sentence level	NLS para.	Word level	NLS para.

Reading comprehension
• Understand how settings influence events and incidents in stories and how they affect characters' behaviour
	2	**Grammatical awareness**
		• Revise and extend work on adjectives from Year 3 Term 2 and link to expressive and figurative language in stories and poetry in particular
		  – examining comparative and superlative adjectives
		  – comparing adjectives on a scale of intensity
			1	**Revision and consolidation from Year 3**
				• Read and spell words through:
				  – identifying syllabic patterns in multi-syllabic words
					1

• Compare and contrast settings across a range of stories; to evaluate, form and justify preferences	3			**Spelling strategies**
				• Use independent spelling strategies, including:
				  – building from other words with similar patterns and meanings
				  – spelling by analogy with other known words
					3

• Understand how the use of expressive and descriptive language can e.g. create moods, arouse expectations, build tension, describe attitudes or emotions	4	**Sentence construction and punctuation**
		• Use the apostrophe accurately to mark possession through:
		  – identifying possessive apostrophes in reading and to whom or what they refer
		  – understanding basic rules for apostrophising singular nouns
		  – distinguishing between uses of the apostrophe for contraction and possession
		  – beginning to use the apostrophe appropriately in their own writing
			2	**Vocabulary extension**
				• Use alternative words and expressions which are more accurate or interesting than the common choices
					9

Writing composition • Develop use of settings in own writing, making use of work on adjectives and figurative language to describe settings effectively	10			• Understand that vocabulary changes over time	11
• Write own examples of descriptive, expressive language based on those read	13				

Grid V Range: Fiction and Poetry, novels, stories and poems by significant children's writers				Year 5 Term 1	
Text level	NLS para.	**Sentence level**	NLS para.	**Word level**	NLS para.
Reading comprehension • Compare the structure of different stories, to discover how they differ in pace, build up, sequence, composition and resolution*	1	**Grammatical awareness** • Understand the difference between direct and indirect speech, e.g. through – finding and comparing examples from reading*	5	**Vocabulary extension** • Explain the differences between synonyms: collect, classify and order sets of words to identify shades of meaning*	7
• Investigate how characters are presented, referring to the text: – through dialogue, action and description* – how the reader responds to them (as victims, heroes etc.)* – through examining their relationships with other characters*	3	– discussing contexts and reasons for using particular forms and their effects* – transforming direct into reported speech and vice-versa, noting changes in punctuation and words that have to be changed or added*		• Use adverbs to qualify verbs in writing dialogue, using a thesaurus to extend vocabulary	10
• Consider how texts can be rooted in the author's experience*	4	**Sentence construction and punctuation**			
• Develop an active attitude towards reading: seeking answers, anticipating events, empathising with characters and imagining events that are described*	9	• Understand the need for punctuation as an aid to the reader, particularly speech marks and commas to mark grammatical boundaries*	6		
• Evaluate a book by referring to details and examples in the text*	10	• From reading, understand how dialogue is set out, e.g. on separate lines for alternative speakers in narrative and the positioning of commas before speech marks*	7		
• Experiment with alternative ways of opening a story using, e.g. description, action, or dialogue*	11	• Revise and extend work on verbs, focusing on – tenses: past tense, present*	8		
• Discuss the enduring appeal of established authors and 'classic' texts	12	– forms: interrogative, active, imperative			
Writing composition • To record their ideas, reflections and predictions about a book, e.g. through a reading log or journal	13				
• Map out texts showing development and structure, e.g. its high and low points, the links between sections, paragraphs, chapters*	14				

interesting use of adjectives and verbs, offering opportunities for vocabulary extension.

It is, of course, important to remember that it is the nature of the story, its timeless qualities, which affects readers most. Few are unmoved by it, and children must be given opportunities for considering how the book makes them think and feel.

When writing *Charlotte's Web*, White undertook extensive research into the life and habits of spiders and it may be appropriate for children to investigate the authenticity of White's information about the animals through use of information books and/or IT texts. A range of reading and writing skills could be developed in this way and comparisons made between the language of different text types.

NB The name Charlotte A Cavatica refers to the current scientific name of the spider in question – Araneus Cavaticus. *Araneae* is the Latin name for spider and was the name of the genus to which Charlotte belonged. Cavaticis is the specific name, altered to agree in gender with Araneus. (The earlier name for the genus was *Epeira*.) The origins of Charlotte's name would provide an interesting starting point for etymological investigations. 'Salutations' is also a Latinate word. See 'word level work' 'Activity 4'.

Text level work

1. Objectives

- To develop an active attitude towards reading: imagining events that are described.
- To consider how the author has used his own experience to create an authentic setting.
- To develop oral skills.

Procedure

- Focus on Chapters 17 and 18 (pp. 126–138) which describe events at the County Fair. Through discussion, establish what information has been incorporated and what this tells the reader about the nature of the fair. Compare this with children's own experience of summer fêtes and draw attention to the author's use of personal experience.
- Children prepare a script for a radio broadcast from the fair, advertising events and reporting them as they happen. Close reference to the text will be necessary. Record broadcast on tape and present to class.
- It would also be possible for children to
  a. create posters advertising the fair
  b. write a report for the local newspaper after the event. Each of these activities would require careful reading of the text, and discussion of the nature of the language – use of tense, differences between spoken and written text, for instance – could follow.
- A possible extension of this work would be to consider elements of the book concerned with farm life and/or the countryside and to draw attention to the detail included. Make links with E. B. White's own experience. (White and his wife, Katherine, bought a farm in rural Maine in 1933 and eventually made it their permanent home in 1957.)

2. Objectives

- To consider the use and impact of a lead question in the opening of a story.
- To show how scene-setting information can be conveyed through dialogue.

2. Procedure

- 'Where's Papa going with that axe?' (p. 7). When first reading the novel to the class, pause after reading this opening line and ask the children what it makes them think about and expect? This will identify some of the connotational meanings within the question which can be focused on later.
- During shared/guided reading, focus on the first page of the novel (p. 7). Draw attention to the extensive use of dialogue and discuss the dramatic impact this has. Transform the opening line into reported speech; write this on a flipchart/board and read it aloud. Discuss the effects of the change. Repeat this with the next two utterances. Emphasise the tension created by the use of direct speech and the way in which characters are introduced in an economical style. Discuss the connotational meanings (e.g. of 'axe') and the effect these have. (NB This will link with described activities at 'sentence level work'.)
- Read the page again (or ask the children to read it) and, on a flipchart or board, list what the author tells the reader. Include setting, character, type of story, e.g.

  Characters
  Fern Arable: girl, aged 8, cares about animals, doesn't know about runts.
  Parents: realistic attitude, farmers, explain to Fern, Mr Arable gentle.
  Setting: rural, springtime, American

- Identify how this information is conveyed (e.g. direct speech, reporting clause, vocabulary, description)
- Photocopy and enlarge the page. Annotate it with points identified during discussion. Use this as a starting point for a display.
- Compare this opening with others which use dialogue. Identify similarities and differences. Annotate and display these examples, e.g. *Eleanor, Elizabeth* by Libby Gleeson, *Mama's Going to Buy You a Mocking Bird* by Jean Little, *Minnie* by Annie M. G. Schmidt.
- Make links with children's own writing: focus on creating openings which start with dialogue.
- During the term consider examples of novels which open in different ways, e.g. a letter, description. Discuss the authors' choices and their effects. Children could be encouraged to collect examples as they read.

3. Objectives

- To develop understanding of the chronological nature and time-scale of the plot.
- To map out the text, showing its structure.

Procedure

- Taking each chapter in turn (or children might work in pairs/groups) identify its time scale, and the nature of events in each.

Draw up a chart to show these.

Chapter	Timescale	Focus
1 2 3	Before breakfast: Spring 5 weeks 2 months after Wilbur's birth: one day in June	Setting scene, introducing main characters Wilbur's early life and relationship with Fern Life in Zuckerman's barn: Wilbur escapes

- When the chart is completed it will be possible to draw a story map to indicate its development and make connections between structure and events. The cyclical aspect of the story will be highlighted, and through discussion, contrasting elements can be identified, e.g. descriptive sections, the climax, periods of action, incidents away from the main thrust of the narrative.

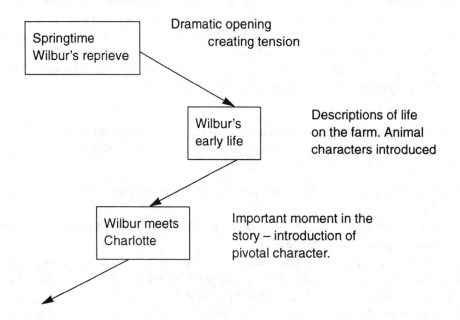

4. Objectives

- To develop understanding of characters and of the different ways in which they are presented.
- To enable children to consider their responses to the characters and the ways in which the author's choices affect and influence their responses.

4a. Procedure

- From your initial discussions, ask the children to tell you what they know and think about one character, e.g. Templeton. Justifying opinions will require reference to the text and should begin to raise awareness of authorial techniques.
- Draw children's attention to these devices for creating characters:
  - dialogue
  - action
  - description

– relationship with others, including what they say about the character – focus on selected extracts which demonstrate the devices, e.g.

Templeton
pp. 32–34 dialogue, description, action
pp. 47–49 action, relationship with others, dialogue, description
pp. 95–98 relationship with others, action, dialogue, description
(pp. 119–120, 133–135, 159–162 in the paperback version).
Choose extracts which show different facets of the character's nature so that children can understand the complexity.

● Draw attention to the vocabulary choices which emphasise character.

Adverbs
'I never do things if I can avoid them,' replied the rat, *sourly* (p. 32)
And Templeton, the rat, crept *stealthily* along the wall (p. 33).

Verbs
'I prefer to spend my time *eating, gnawing, spying* and *hiding*' (p. 32)
Templeton *was* down there now, *rummaging* around (p. 96)
Templeton *crouched* under the straw at the bottom of the crate (p. 150).

● Consider responses to the character in the light of what seems to be the author's view.
● How do other characters view the one being focused on?
● Summarise the main points which have been identified.

NB The children could explore this aspect further in independent activities at sentence and word level.

4b. Procedure

● From previous investigations, children create a character portrait. This might take the form of:
  – a prose description
  – a poster with speech bubbles in which children write observations by different characters based on evidence collected. This could be illustrated in some way.

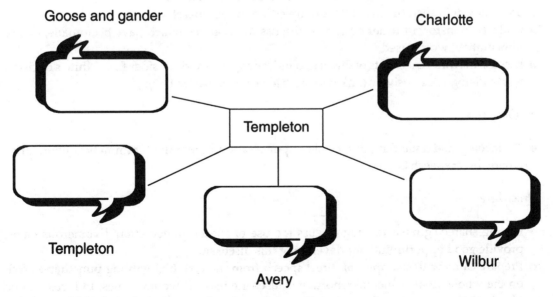

Goose and gander

Charlotte

Templeton

Templeton

Avery

Wilbur

This would link with 'sentence level work' on direct speech.

Sentence level work

1. Objectives

- To develop understanding of the difference between direct and indirect speech.
- To develop awareness of the punctuation associated with direct speech and of the layout of dialogue in narrative text.

Procedure

- Select an extract in which there is sustained use of dialogue (e.g. p. 52).
- During shared/guided reading, draw attention to the layout of the dialogue, i.e. separate lines for different speakers, and to the punctuation used to separate speech from reporting clauses.
- Prepare cards with examples from the selected page. Highlight speech in some way, e.g. underlining or different colour.

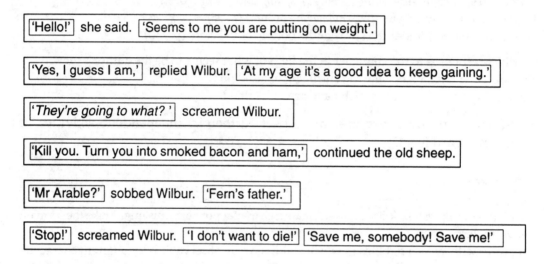

'Hello!' she said. 'Seems to me you are putting on weight'.

'Yes, I guess I am,' replied Wilbur. 'At my age it's a good idea to keep gaining.'

'They're going to what?' screamed Wilbur.

'Kill you. Turn you into smoked bacon and ham,' continued the old sheep.

'Mr Arable?' sobbed Wilbur. 'Fern's father.'

'Stop!' screamed Wilbur. 'I don't want to die!' 'Save me, somebody! Save me!'

- Discuss the punctuation used and how this aids the reader.
- Show how to transform one of the examples into direct speech.
- Children transform further examples: discuss the changes which have been made, e.g. of punctuation, words used.
- Discuss the different effects of direct and indirect speech and consider E. B. White's decision to use dialogue extensively (link with 'text level work', Activity 2).

2. Objective

- To develop understanding of the role of punctuation in marking grammatical boundaries where direct speech is used.

Procedure

- During shared/guided reading discuss the use of speech punctuation. (Numerous pages provide good opportunities for developing this discussion.)
- Prepare cards with examples of direct speech from the text, highlighting punctuation (NB on the whole, final or medial reporting clauses are used. It would be best to focus on one type initially to avoid confusion.)

Final reporting clauses

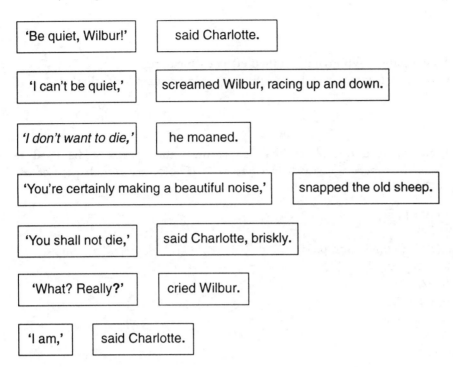

- Consider the cards with direct speech on. Discuss the punctuation and its positioning; focus particularly on commas.
- Using different examples from the text, from which the punctuation has been omitted, children should work in pairs to:
  - match direct speech with final reporting clause;
  - add the appropriate punctuation.

(NB Cards could be re-used if they are laminated and a water-based pen used.)

3. Objective

- To revise work on verbs, focusing on the use of present and past tenses in descriptive passages.

Procedure

- Photocopy selected extracts. (Openings of chapters provide useful examples, e.g. Chapters 3, 4, 6, 9, 11.)
- Working in pairs, children should highlight or underline the verbs and identify the tense used.
- Discuss the author's use of present or past tense in these passages and the resulting effects, (e.g. the opening paragraph of Chapter 6 includes both present and past tense).
- Ask children to transform verbs in selected passages from past to present tense, or vice versa, and discuss the necessary changes and resulting effects. (NB The opening page of *The Way to Sattin Shore* by Philippa Pearce is an interesting example of an author using present and past tenses to create a particular effect, and this could be used as a comparison.

Word level work

1. Objectives

- To develop understanding of synonyms and their effect on meaning.
- To extend children's use of synonyms when writing reporting clauses for dialogue.

Procedure

- During shared/guided reading, ask children to identify the speech verbs used as alternatives to 'said' in reporting clauses in Chapter 7. (Photocopy the chapter or use multiple copies.) They are:

  she *replied* (Charlotte, p. 51)
  replied Wilbur (p. 52)
  screamed Wilbur (p.52, (3 times) and p. 54)
  continued the old sheep (p. 52)
  sobbed Wilbur (p. 52)
  he *moaned* (Wilbur, p. 53)
  snapped the old sheep (p. 54)
  cried Wilbur (p. 54)
  asked Wilbur (p. 54)

List them on a flip chart or board. Discuss what each word conveys, including the information revealed about characters.

- Children work in pairs to repeat this activity with other designated chapters. NB Most chapters reveal interesting points but you might like to begin with Chapters 5, 6, 10 and 20.
- Children report back to the class. Discuss the range of words used, and their effects.
- Display the list of speech verbs so that children can be encouraged to extend the range used in their own writing. This list can be added to as children find other examples in their own reading.

NB An extension of this activity, at word level, would be to find synonyms for some of the verbs and discuss shades and variations of meaning within them, e.g.

asked	demanded
	enquired
	questioned
	queried
	requested
screamed	yelled
	shrieked
	bawled
	squealed
	screeched

2. Objective

- To develop understanding of synonyms and shades of meaning.

Procedure

- Read aloud the opening paragraph of Chapter 7, in which White expresses views about flies. Draw attention to the following three verbs:

  The cows *hated* them
  The horses *detested* them
  The sheep *loathed* them

  Discuss the shades of meaning embedded in these three words and the order in which they would be placed to indicate increased strength of feeling.

- Write each word on a separate card. Ask the children to think of further synonyms, e.g. disliked, despised. Use a thesaurus to find alternatives and write all the new words on cards.
- Ask the children to order the set of words collected and discuss shades of meaning.

3. Objectives

- To explore the use of unusual vocabulary choices.
- To develop children's awareness of how context affects meaning.

Procedure

- During shared/guided reading, draw children's attention to words which have been used in interesting or unusual ways, e.g.

  'No I only *distribute* pigs to early risers,' said Mr Arable (p. 10)
  'Fern was up at daylight, trying to rid the world of *injustice*' (p. 10)
  '*Reconsider, reconsider!*' cried the goose (p. 23)
  'Rain fell in the barnyard and ran in crooked *courses* down into the lane . . .' (p. 25)
  'Skim milk, crusts, *middlings*, bits of doughnut . . .' (p. 25)
  'Talking with Templeton was not the most interesting *occupation* in the world . . .' (p. 26)
  '. . . came a small voice he had never heard before. It sounded rather *thin*, but pleasant.' (p. 35)
  'Will the *party* who *addressed me* at bedtime last night kindly speak up.' (p. 38)
  'I *beg* everyone's *pardon*,' whispered Wilbur. 'I didn't mean to be *objectionable*.' (p. 38)
  '*Salutations!*' said the voice. (p. 39)
  'It's a *miserable inheritance*,' said Wilbur, gloomily. (p. 43).

- Discuss their meanings in these contexts, using a dictionary if necessary, comparing them with children's previous understanding.
- Children could search for further examples of unfamiliar words and/or words used in unusual ways, and research the meanings created.

4. Objective

- To develop children's understanding of denotational and connotational meanings of words.

Procedure

- Prepare cards with the 'web words' on

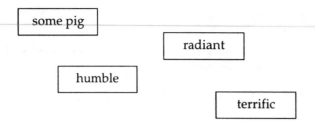

Ask the children to research dictionary definitions of these words: discuss.

- Discuss the connotational meanings of the words and their significance in
  - events in the story
  - creating symbolic meanings
- Select further interesting or unusual words for consideration, e.g.

Salutations	(p. 39)
trapper	(p. 43)
miracle	(p. 78)
gamble	(p. 44)
lair	(p. 50)
anaesthetic	(p. 51)
conspiracy	(p. 52)
idiosyncracy	(p. 86)

Conclusion

Nurturing children's confidence in their literacy acquisition is crucial if we are to develop enthusiastic and critical adult readers and writers; hence choosing appropriate texts as a stimulus for learning is a priority.

Teachers who have piloted the NLS have found that recognising the potential for developing text, sentence and word level knowledge, through good children's literature, is an important aspect of planning for the Literacy Hour. Tasks linked and structured to ongoing work on texts, including sentence and word level work, are given a context, and highlight for children important decisions that writers make for readers. Time allocated to examining texts alongside developing familiarisation with the framework is particularly necessary within the first year of the project in order to consider planning for the range of texts to be used throughout Key Stages 1 and 2.

We are aware that we have only been able to discuss a limited number of fiction and poetry texts. Non-fiction is a huge area for investigation and we felt unable to do it justice within this book. Other important types of fiction and poetry, such as picture books for older children have not been included; however similar methods of planning would be appropriate. We hope that we have shown that good texts have the potential to cover many of the NLS objectives. Our activities therefore are not programmes of work around particular texts, but ideas that could be used across a range of fiction and poetry. It is important to remember that some objectives should be taught in other contexts and without reference to these texts, so that spurious connections are not made.

When planning whole-class, group or individual work, objectives should be clearly focused, few in number and appropriate to the children's ongoing development of reading and writing skills. Clarity in the purpose and nature of tasks, linked to objectives, will help in the monitoring and assessment of children's progress throughout each term.

Bibliography

Agard, J. (1993) 'If Only I Could Take Home a Snowflake', in *I Din Do Nuttin*. London: Random House.

Agard, J. and Nichols, G. (1991) *No Hickory No Dickory No Dock*. London: Viking.

Ahlberg, J. and A. (1980) *Funnybones*. London: Heinemann.

Ahlberg, J. and A. (1986) *The Jolly Postman*. London: Heinemann.

Alborough, J. (1994) *It's the Bear*. London: Walker Books.

Ardizzone, E. (1980) *English Fairy Tales*. London: André Deutsch.

Baum, L. (1984) *I Want to See the Moon*. London: Methuen.

Benton, M. and Fox, G. (1985) *Teaching Literature Nine to Fourteen*. Oxford: Oxford University Press.

Berenstein, S. and J. (1972) *Bears in the Night*. London: Collins.

Bettleheim, B. (1979) *The Uses of Enchantment*. London: Penguin.

Biro, V. (1998) *Goldilocks and the Three Bears*. Oxford: Oxford University Press.

Briggs, R. (1973) *Jim and the Beanstalk*. London: Puffin.

Briggs, R. (1974) *The Fairy Tale Treasury*. London: Puffin.

Briggs, R. (1994) *The Bear*. London: Julia Macrae.

Bryant, P. and Bradley, L. (1985) *Children's Reading Problems*. Oxford: Basil Blackwell.

Brownjohn, S. (1980) *Does it Have to Rhyme?* London: Hodder & Stoughton.

Brownjohn, S. (1982) *What Rhymes with 'Secret'?* London: Hodder & Stoughton.

Brownjohn, S. (1989) *The Ability to Name Cats*. London: Hodder & Stoughton.

Burningham, J. (1970) *Mr Gumpy's Motor Car*. London: Jonathan Cape.

Burningham, J. (1970) *Mr Gumpy's Outing*. London: Jonathan Cape.

Butterfield, M. (1998) *Goldilocks*. London: Heinemann.

Butterworth, N. (1992) *Jasper's Beanstalk*. Kent: Hodder & Stoughton.

Campbell, R. (1982) *Dear Zoo*. Middlesex: Picture Puffin.

Chambers, A. (1994) *Tell Me; Children, Reading and Talk*. Stroud: Thimble Press.

Charles, F. (1991) *The Kiskadee Queen*. London: Blackie.

Crossley-Holland, K. (1987) *British Folk Tales*. London: Orchard Books.

Dahl, R. (1984) *Revolting Rhymes*. London: Puffin.

Daley, A. (1994) *Jack and the Beanstalk*. London: Ladybird.

de Beer, H. (1996) *Little Polar Bear, Take me Home!* London: North-South Books.

de la Mare, W. (1947) *Collected Stories for Children*, (Dick and the Beanstalk). London: Faber.

DES (1989) *Report of the English Working Party 5–16*. London: HMSO.

DfEE (1998) *The National Literacy Strategy*. London: DfEE.

Dunne, J. *et al* (1987) *In Tune with Yourself?* Cambridge: Cambridge University Press.

Edwards, H. (1991) *There's a Hippopotamus on the Roof*. London: Picture Knight.

Evans, C. S. (1972) *Cinderella*. London: Heinemann.

Fatchen, M. (1990) 'Children Lost', in *Poems Not to be Missed*. S. Hill and D. Strauss (eds). Australia: Magic Bean.

Gadsby, D. and Harrop, B. (eds) (1981) *Harlequin*. London: A. & C. Black.

Galdone, P. (1973) *Little Red Hen*. Tadworth: World's Work.

Garner, A. (1993) *Jack and the Beanstalk*. London: Picture Books.

Gleeson, L. (1984) *Eleanor Elizabeth*. Middlesex: Puffin.

Gliori, D. (1996) *Mr Bear to the Rescue*. London: Orchard Books.

Goswami, U. and Bryant, P. (1990) *Phonological Skills and Learning to Read*. Hove: Lawrence Erlbaum Associates.

Harrop, B. (1976) *Okki-Takki-Unga*. London: A. & C. Black.

Hawkins, C. (1990) *This is the House that Jack Built*. London: Heinemann.

Hayes, S. and Craig, H. (1980) *This is the Bear and the Scary Night*. London: Walker Books.

Hayes, S. (1988) *This is the Bear and the Picnic Lunch*. London: Walker Books.

Hayes, S. (1988) *This is the Bear*. London: Walker Books.

Hoberman, M. A. (1986) *A House is a House for Me*. London: Puffin.

Howe, J. (1989) *Jack and the Beanstalk*. London: Little, Brown.

Hutchins, P. (1968) *Rosie's Walk*. London: Bodley Head.

Hutchins, P. (1994) *The Wind Blew*. London: Red Fox.

Impey, R. and Beck, I. (1992) *Orchard Book of Fairy Tales*. London: Orchard Books.

Inkpen, M. (1992) *Threadbear*. Kent: Hodder & Stoughton.

James, S. (1991) *Dear Greenpeace*. London: Walker Books.

Kerr, J. (1983) *Mog in the Dark*. London: Collins.

Kitamura, S. (1986) *When Sheep Cannot Sleep*. Harlow: Oliver & Boyd.

Langley, J. (1991) *The Three Bears and Goldilocks*. London: Harper Collins.

Little, J. (1984) *Mama's Going to Buy You a Mocking Bird*. Middlesex: Penguin.

Lurie, A. (1991) *Cap o' Rushes*. Northampton: BBC Books.

McNaughton, C. (1993) *ABC and Things*. Pan Macmillan Children's Books.

Maris, R. (1984) *Are You There Bear?* London: Julia Macrae.

Matterson, E. (1991) *This Little Puffin*. London: Puffin.

Murphy, J. (1980) *Peace at Last*. London: Macmillan.

Murphy, J. (1983) *Whatever Next?* London: Macmillan.

Nash, O. (1990) 'The Adventures of Isabel', in *Poems Not to be Missed*. S. Hill and D. Strauss (eds). Australia: Magic Bean.

Nimmo, J. (1993) *The Starlight Cloak*. London: Collins.

Noonan, D. (1995) *The Best-Loved Bear*. Southam: Scholastic.

Noyes, A. (1981) *The Highwayman*. Illustrated by Charles Keeping. Oxford: Oxford University Press.

Oakley, G. (1990) *Once Upon a Time*. London: Macmillan.

Opie, I. and P. (1967) *The Lore and Language of School Children*. London: Clarendon.

Parkes, B. (1989) *Goodnight, Goodnight*. Illustrated by T. Denton. Victoria, Australia: Mimosa Publications.

Pearce, P. (1983) *The Way to Sattin Shore*. London: Puffin.

Philip, N. (1992) *Penguin Book of English Folktales*. London: Penguin.

Prelutsky, J. (1983) *The Walker Book of Poetry*. London: Walker Books.

Rosen, M. (1993) *We're Going on a Bear Hunt*. London: Walker Books.

Rosen, M. (1995) *Walking the Bridge of Your Nose*. London: Kingfisher.

Ross, T. (1980) *Jack and the Beanstalk*. London: Puffin.

Ross, T. (1991) *Jack and the Beanstalk*. London: Anderson Press.

Sansom, C. (1974) *Speech Rhymes*. London: A. & C. Black.

Schmidt, A. M. G. (1992) *Minnie*. Stroud: Turton & Chambers.

Selway, M. (1994) *Wish You Were Here*. London: Stanley Paul.

Steptoe, J. (1991) *Mufaro's Beautiful Daughters*. London: Hodder & Stoughton.

Tolstoy, A. and Oxenbury, H. (1972) *The Great Big Enormous Turnip*. London: Pan Books.

Townsend, H. (1990) *The Deathwood Letters*. London: Red Fox.

Vipoint, A. (1971) *The Elephant and the Bad Baby*. Harmondsworth: Puffin.

Waddell, M. (1990) *Class Three and the Beanstalk*. London: Puffin.

Waddell, M. and Barton, J. (1992) *The Pig in the Pond*. London: Walker Books.

Waddell, M. and Firth, B. (1989) *Can't You Sleep Little Bear?* London: Walker Books.

Waddell, M. and Firth, B. (1994) *The Big Big Sea*. London: Walker Books.

White, E. B. (1952) *Charlotte's Web*. London: Puffin.

Wildsmith, B. (1994) *Jack and the Meanstalk*. Oxford: Oxford University Press.

Index